Urban Informatics

Information shapes urban spaces in ways that most people rarely stop to consider. From data-driven planning to grassroots activism to influencing the routes we walk, bike, and drive, new information technologies are helping city dwellers to leverage information in new ways. These technologies shape the uses and character of urban spaces. Information technologies and tools such as social media and GIS tracking applications are being used by individuals as they go about their daily lives, not as alternatives to social interaction, but as opportunities to participate in the shared experience of urban life.

This edited volume focuses on the creative application and management of information technologies in urban environments, with an emphasis on the intersection between citizen participation in creating city environments and the policy-making that supports it. The chapters address critical issues including the digital divide, transportation planning, use of public spaces, community building, and local events. This book was originally published as a special issue of the *Journal of Urban Technology*.

Kristene Unsworth is an Assistant Professor in the College of Computing and Informatics at Drexel University, Philadelphia, Pennsylvania, USA. Her research, as well as her teaching, focuses on information policy and ethics.

Andrea Forte is an Assistant Professor in the College of Computing and Informatics at Drexel University, Philadelphia, Pennsylvania, USA. She studies and designs technologies that support collaboration, cooperation, and learning in a variety of contexts.

Richardson Dilworth is an Associate Professor of Political Science, and Director of the Center for Public Policy, at Drexel University, Philadelphia, Pennsylvania, USA. His research and teaching both focus on American urban political development, urban environment policy, and community economic development.

Urban Informatics
Collaboration at the nexus of policy, technology and design, people and data

Edited by
Kristene Unsworth, Andrea Forte and Richardson Dilworth

LONDON AND NEW YORK

First published 2016
by Routledge
2 Park Square, Milton Park, Abingdon, Oxon, OX14 4RN, UK

and by Routledge
711 Third Avenue, New York, NY 10017, USA

Routledge is an imprint of the Taylor & Francis Group, an informa business

© 2016 The Society of Urban Technology

All rights reserved. No part of this book may be reprinted or reproduced or utilised in any form or by any electronic, mechanical, or other means, now known or hereafter invented, including photocopying and recording, or in any information storage or retrieval system, without permission in writing from the publishers.

Trademark notice: Product or corporate names may be trademarks or registered trademarks, and are used only for identification and explanation without intent to infringe.

British Library Cataloguing in Publication Data
A catalogue record for this book is available from the British Library

ISBN 13: 978-1-138-11949-9

Typeset in Palatino
by RefineCatch Limited, Bungay, Suffolk

Publisher's Note
The publisher accepts responsibility for any inconsistencies that may have arisen during the conversion of this book from journal articles to book chapters, namely the possible inclusion of journal terminology.

Disclaimer
Every effort has been made to contact copyright holders for their permission to reprint material in this book. The publishers would be grateful to hear from any copyright holder who is not here acknowledged and will undertake to rectify any errors or omissions in future editions of this book.

Contents

Citation Information vii
Notes on Contributors ix

Introduction – Urban Informatics: The Role of Citizen Participation in Policy Making 1
Kristene Unsworth, Andrea Forte, and Richardson Dilworth

1. From Design Fiction to Design Friction: Speculative and Participatory 7
   Laura Forlano and Anijo Mathew

2. Technology-Enabled Participatory Platforms for Civic Engagement: The Case of U.S. Cities 25
   Kevin C. Desouza and Akshay Bhagwatwar

3. Potential and Challenges for Social media in the Neighbourhood Context 51
   Bonnie J. Johnson and Germaine R. Halegoua

4. The Digital Divide in Citizen-Initiated Government Contacts: A GIS Approach 77
   Sara Cavallo, Joann Lynch, and Peter Scull

5. Does Anything Ever Happen Around Here? Assessing the Online Information Landscape for Local Events 95
   Claudia López, Brian Butler, and Peter Brusilovsky

6. Goals, Challenges, and Capacity of Regional Data Portals in the United States: An Updated Understanding of Long-Standing Discussions 125
   Joanna P. Ganning, Sarah L. Coffin, Benjamin McCall, and Kathleen Carson

Index 141

Citation Information

The chapters in this book were originally published in the *Journal of Urban Technology*, volume 21, issue 4 (October 2014). When citing this material, please use the original page numbering for each article, as follows:

Introduction
From the Guest Editors: Urban Informatics: The Role of Citizen Participation in Policy Making
Kristene Unsworth, Andrea Forte and Richardson Dilworth
Journal of Urban Technology, volume 21, issue 4 (October 2014) pp. 1–6

Chapter 1
From Design Fiction to Design Friction: Speculative and Participatory Design of Values-Embedded Urban Technology
Laura Forlano and Anijo Mathew
Journal of Urban Technology, volume 21, issue 4 (October 2014) pp. 7–24

Chapter 2
Technology-Enabled Participatory Platforms for Civic Engagement: The Case of U.S. Cities
Kevin C. Desouza and Akshay Bhagwatwar
Journal of Urban Technology, volume 21, issue 4 (October 2014) pp. 25–50

Chapter 3
Potential and Challenges for Social Media in the Neighborhood Context
Bonnie J. Johnson and Germaine R. Halegoua
Journal of Urban Technology, volume 21, issue 4 (October 2014) pp. 51–76

Chapter 4
The Digital Divide in Citizen-Initiated Government Contacts: A GIS Approach
Sara Cavallo, Joann Lynch, and Peter Scull
Journal of Urban Technology, volume 21, issue 4 (October 2014) pp. 77–94

Chapter 5
Does Anything Ever Happen Around Here? Assessing the Online Information Landscape for Local Events
Claudia López, Brian Butler and Peter Brusilovsky
Journal of Urban Technology, volume 21, issue 4 (October 2014) pp. 95–124

CITATION INFORMATION

Chapter 6
Goals, Challenges, and Capacity of Regional Data Portals in the United States: An Updated Understanding of Long-Standing Discussions
Joanna P. Ganning, Sarah L. Coffin, Benjamin McCall, and Kathleen Carson
Journal of Urban Technology, volume 21, issue 4 (October 2014) pp. 125–139

For any permission-related enquiries please visit:
http://www.tandfonline.com/page/help/permissions

Notes on Contributors

Akshay Bhagwatwar is a doctoral candidate and associate instructor in the Department of Operations and Decision Technologies, Kelley School of Business, at Indiana University, Bloomington, IN, USA.

Peter Brusilovsky is a Professor of Information Science and Intelligent Systems at the University of Pittsburgh, PA, USA, where he also directs the Personalized AdaptiveWeb Systems lab.

Brian S. Butler is a Professor in the College of Information Studies at the University of Maryland, College Park, MD, USA, and the Director of the Center for the Advanced Study of Communities and Information. His work focuses on the interplay between technology and organizing.

Kathleen Carson is a doctoral candidate in the Department of Public Policy Studies at Saint Louis University, MO, USA. Her research focuses on environmental policy.

Sara Cavallo is a graduate student at Pennsylvania State University, State College, PA, USA.

Sarah L. Coffin is an Associate Professor of Urban Planning and real estate development in the Center for Sustainability at Saint Louis University, MO, USA. Her current research focuses on the role that evidence plays in driving policy decisions and how science informs the policy debate around local industrial land use decisions.

Kevin C. Desouza is Associate Dean for Research, and Professor in the School of Public Affairs, at Arizona State University, Phoenix, AZ, USA.

Richardson Dilworth is an Associate Professor of Political Science, and Director of the Center for Public Policy, at Drexel University, Philadelphia, Pennsylvania, USA. His research and teaching both focus on American urban political development, urban environment policy, and community economic development.

Laura Forlano is an Assistant Professor of Design at the Institute of Design at Illinois Institute of Technology, Chicago, IL, USA, where she is the founder of the Critical Futures Lab. Her research is on emergent forms of organizing and urbanism enabled by mobile, wireless, and ubiquitous computing technologies with an emphasis on the sociotechnical practices and spaces of innovation.

Andrea Forte is an Assistant Professor in the College of Computing and Informatics at Drexel University, Philadelphia, Pennsylvania, USA. She studies and designs technologies that support collaboration, cooperation, and learning in a variety of contexts.

Joanna P. Ganning is an Assistant Professor in the Department of City & Metropolitan Planning, and the executive director of the Metropolitan Research Center, at the University of Utah, Salt Lake City, UT, USA. Her research focuses quantitatively on place-based economic development, natural resources, and the interface between the two.

Germaine R. Halegoua is an Assistant Professor in the Department of Film and Media studies at the University of Kansas, Manhattan, KS, USA.

Bonnie J. Johnson is an Associate Professor in the Department of Urban Planning at the University of Kansas, Manhattan, KS, USA.

Claudia Lopez is a Ph.D. student in the School of Information Sciences at the University of Pittsburgh, PA, USA. She studies how information is disseminated, sought for, and discovered both online and offline, in urban settings.

Joann Lynch has a BA in Geography from Colgate University, Hamilton, NY, USA. She is currently a research analyst at a primary research firm.

Anijo Punnen Mathew is an Associate Professor at the Institute of Design at Illinois Institute of Technology, Chicago, IL, USA. His research looks at developing strategies for companies to adapt and change as we move from an industrial economy to an information economy, and at evaluating new semantic appropriations of place as enabled by technology and media convergence.

Ben McCall holds a Master of Arts in urban planning and real estate development from Saint Louis University, MO, USA, and works at America's Central Port as a planner.

Peter Scull is an Associate Professor of Geography at Colgate University, Hamilton, NY, USA.

Kristene Unsworth is an Assistant Professor in the College of Computing and Informatics at Drexel University, Philadelphia, Pennsylvania, USA. Her research, as well as her teaching, focuses on information policy and ethics.

Urban Informatics: The Role of Citizen Participation in Policy Making

Kristene Unsworth, Andrea Forte, and Richardson Dilworth

This special issue of the *Journal of Urban Technology* highlights the rich scholarship and activity in the arena of urban informatics. The issue includes selected papers from the *Symposium on Urban Informatics* as well as accepted submissions that are thematically relevant to this collection. The *Symposium on Urban Informatics* was held at Drexel University in June 2013. The goal of the event was to bring together designers, city planners and managers, technologists, scholars, and entrepreneurs working at the nexus of policy, technology, design, and data. Advances in technologies that have the potential to empower and engage individuals require a high degree of collaboration between academic researchers, municipal employees, private sector visionaries, and the general public. The articles in this issue are focused on North American urban spaces and are only a sampling of the ongoing and exciting work happening not only in the academic arena, but throughout our urban environments.

Definition of Urban Informatics

The US Census classifies as "urban" as "all territory, population, and housing units located within urbanized areas and urban clusters" (US Census, 2014). Urbanized areas are represented by "densely developed territory that contains 50,000 or more people," while urban clusters are "densely developed territory that has at least 2,500 people but fewer than 50,000 people." In the 2010 Census, nearly 250 million individuals in the United States lived in urban areas (US Census Bureau, 2010 Census). Considering that the total US population at the time of the 2010 Census was over 308 million, 80 percent of the population can be said to live in an urban area or cluster. The urban environment is complex and many new technologies offer opportunities for city dwellers to interact with each other and their environment.

Urban informatics is about the modern human experience of city life (Foth et al., 2011). Computing is essential to that experience as ubiquitous technologies and unprecedented forms and amounts of data make possible new ways of interacting with each other and our urban environments. Cities, as points of concentrated social and economic activity that also often reflect, in extreme form, conflicts and inequalities (Foth et al., 2011), provide a challenging context for human-centered research and design that takes into account not only the technological, but the social, political, and human features of possible urban futures. Urban informatics is about *people*, *place*, and *technology*.

Information technologies have become tools that enable city residents to participate in renegotiating and redefining urban spaces. This special issue focuses on the creative application and management of information technologies in urban environments with an emphasis on the intersection between civic participation and policy-making. The articles address critical issues including digital divides, transportation planning, the use of public spaces, community building, and local events.

Although information technologies and social media, in particular, are sometimes framed as alternatives to physical interaction and co-location, articles in this collection highlight the ways that information technologies become intertwined with physical spaces.

Implications of this Definition: Understanding Borders

"The City" cannot be defined as a singular entity. Each city or urban area is made up of smaller units—such as neighborhoods, blocks, council districts, wards, or school districts—each inhabited by individuals with particular needs and expectations (Foth et al., 2011). The papers in this volume examine processes by which the shared space that is a city becomes a kind of *place*. Harrison and Dourish (1996: 67) explain that *space* describes the three-dimensional physical structure within which interactions can occur, whereas a *place* also refers to the meaning that a particular space has taken on for the people who inhabit it; in other words, "Space is the opportunity, place is the understood reality." In the papers that follow, we find examples of how governments, groups, and individuals use technologies to define a diverse array of urban places.

Contributions

The original call for participation in the *Symposium* invited submissions that examined processes at the nexus of policy, technology and design, people, and data. In their paper, Forlano and Mathew discuss the idea of codesign workshops as a means of communicating across local borders. The article represents the result of workshops on urban technology held in Chicago, New York, and Boston during 2012-2013. These events demonstrate how local groups and individuals interface with local governments to inform policy for urban spaces. Digital technologies are an integral part of urban space and challenge traditional separations between global and local or private and public. They introduce a "codesign toolkit" for urban technology that can be used by policymakers to closely examine the relationships among people, technology, and place.

Participation and engagement are also themes in Desouza's examination of technology-enabled participatory platforms. Desouza presents four main archetypes of technology-enabled participatory platforms: citizen-centric/citizen data, citizen-centric/government data, government-centric/citizen data, and government-centric/government data. While Forlano and Mathew discuss *codesign*, Desouza finds that the platforms introduced are not the product of collaborative efforts between citizens and public agencies. Some of the platforms were initially developed in response to lapses in government and agency service provision. The platforms discussed by Desouza are successful within the communities they are being used, yet still may mirror some problems present in other aspects of technology use and public services; namely, that the services (or platforms) are not available equality to all citizens. Economic issues, access to the platforms and/or to the smart phone technology on which the platforms run as well as other demographic factors all influence the reach of these public platforms.

In their article, Johnson and Halegoua bring into focus the meaning of "neighborhood" in the digital age and how it may affect traditional understandings of the neighborhood association. Social media tools are touted as the *de facto* means for sharing information. Johnson and Halegoua examine this assumption in relation to communication needs within a neighborhood. They examine both the use and non-use of social media for community organizing. In the neighborhood they studied, the use of social media was unsuccessful in reengaging community members with a local community association. For this community, face-to-face interaction and off-line relationships play a significant role in neighborhood association activities. The findings demonstrate that non-participation cannot be remedied merely by plugging in new technologies; furthermore, information technologies, when used, must be designed and implemented in ways that support and complement residents' use and their understanding of the role IT plays in their lives and communities.

While Johnson and Halegoua discuss the importance of recognizing on- and off-line relationships in community organizing, Cavallo discusses the way 311 services provide citizens with direct access to local government. Based on analysis of data from three cities: New York, San Francisco, and Washington, DC; citizen-generated data in the form of voluntary geographic information (VGI) provides citizens with a way to participate and be empowered to solve community issues. This represents what Cavallo refers to as "third wave e-gov" or c2g2c. In spite of this engagement, this article suggests that there may be a digital divide in participation and that the demographic profile of a city plays a role in e-Government. An interesting result is that for the data examined, higher educated citizens with children are *less* likely to participate and ask questions via 311. As in earlier articles, questions need to be asked about who actually uses technology-enabled tools to interact with government agencies. Why do some people actively use these technologies and others continue to connect face to face or through traditional tools. Additionally, we must still ask if these tools do in fact reach urban denizens who have been traditionally left out of the conversation—namely the poor.

Participation in city and neighborhood activities isn't only related to 311 problems and needs. Lopez and Butler assess the online information landscape of local events. Historically, communities have used town square bulletin boards, newsletters, and traditional media to advertise local events. The ubiquity of online information via web sites and social media offers new opportunities to advertise and potentially reach an expanded audience. Lopez and Butler find that although the technologies provide a means to promote local events, the diversity of web sites and social media tools cover only a limited portion of events and no single technology gives a cohesive account of what events are available for community members on any given date.

While it can be said that technology provides the opportunity for increased participation in urban affairs, there is still a need to marry traditional forms of interaction with online tools and technology. In many cases the intended audience is not the public at large, but the individuals who work directly with the systems that make up and provide the data from the infrastructure of our urban environment. In their paper, Ganning, Coffin, McCall, and Carson provide a review of the current state of regional data portals in the United States and question if the sites now available meet the needs of planning and public administration processes. The paper is directed at both academics and practitioners who design and work with regional data portals. The article is intended to help guide those involved with planning data portals as well as their collaborators: universities, regional governments, and municipalities.

Acknowledgments

The articles which make up this special issue are largely the result of the *Symposium on Urban Informatics* held at Drexel University in Philadelphia, PA on June 10, 2013. We would like to acknowledge the generous support of Drexel's College of Computing and Informatics as well as the Center for Public Policy in making the *Symposium* a success. The Expressive and Creative Interaction Technologies (ExCITe) research center on the Drexel campus deserves special thanks for hosting this event. We would like to thank all of the participants of the symposium for their insightful contributions on the topic of urban informatics as we experience today as well as our visions for the future. We would like to offer specific thanks to Richard Hanley, editor-in-chief of *The Journal of Urban Technology*, for taking time to attend the symposium itself and his support in making this special issue a reality.

Bibliography

M. Foth, J.H. Choi, and C. Satchell, "Urban Informatics," in *CSCW 2011* (Hangzhao, China: ACM, 2011).

S. Harrison, and P. Dourish, "Re-Place-ing Space?: The Roles of Place and Space in Collaborative Systems," *Proceedings of the 1996 ACM Conference on Computer Supported Cooperative Work*, 7 (1996) 67–76. doi:10.1145/240080.240193

U.S. Census Bureau, *Geography: Urban and Rural Classification* (Washington, DC: Government Printing Office. U.S. Census Bureau. 2012).

From Design Fiction to Design Friction: Speculative and Participatory Design of Values-Embedded Urban Technology

Laura Forlano and Anijo Mathew

ABSTRACT *This paper discusses the results of the Designing Policy project, which engages current debates about urban technology through the creation of a visual toolkit and a series of workshops. The workshops were held in Chicago, New York, and Boston during 2012–2013 with funding from the Urban Communication Foundation. The purpose of the project was three-fold: (1) to open up the "black box" of urban technology in order to reveal the politics embedded in city infrastructures; (2) to move beyond discussions of urban problems and solutions, and towards a more conceptual future-oriented space; and (3) to explore the use of design methods such as visual prototypes and participatory design. This article introduces the concept of design friction as a way of understanding the ways in which conflicts, tensions and disagreements can move complex socio-technical discussions forward where they can be worked out through material engagement in hands-on prototyping.*

Introduction

In recent years, cities around the world have embraced the Smart City agenda, one that technology companies such as Cisco and IBM promise will result in greater productivity, efficiency, innovation, and security for citizens. Through the widespread deployment of information technology—cameras in adaptive traffic signals, networked parking meters with dynamic pricing, and sensors embedded in garbage cans—cities are redesigning their infrastructures and, at the same time, making critical decisions about the kinds of citizens that can participate in urban life. For the majority of citizens, technology remains as a "black box" with little attention to the implicit social, cultural, political, and economic implications of any given technology decision on the experience of living, working and, more generally, belonging in cities. In tandem with these top-down efforts to roll-out urban technologies, cities have become hosts to a variety of more bottom-up civic hackathons and participatory workshops that aim to find technological solutions to urban problems. There have been a number of significant critiques of the

Smart City agenda, which aim to open up alternative lines of inquiry about the opportunities and risks of urban technologies (Greenfield, 2013; Townsend, 2013).

This paper discusses the results of the Designing Policy project, which engages current debates about Smart Cities through the creation of a visual toolkit and the design of series of workshops. The primary motivation for the project was to open up the "black box" of urban technology in order to reveal the politics, ethics, and values that are embedded in city infrastructures. For example, the use of parking meters with dynamic pricing may unfairly penalize a particular group of citizens with the common necessity of finding parking in a particular neighborhood at a particular time of day by requiring that they pay a higher price. This is merely an example of the implications of relying on algorithmic forms of management and control over city resources such as parking. Without a careful examination of (and public deliberation around) the opportunities, risks, and unintended consequences present within urban technological systems, policymakers may inadvertently be designing cities that benefit a very small minority of citizens while ignoring the majority. The introduction of a wider set of values—beyond productivity, efficiency, innovation, and security—that might more accurately represent the everyday lives of citizens has the potential to inform current discussions around Smart Cities as well as the decisions that policymakers ultimately will make about the adoption, deployment, and use of (or rejection of) urban technologies in their cities.

A secondary motivation for this project was to move beyond discussions of urban problems and solutions, and towards a more generative future-oriented space of speculation informed by the everyday lives of citizens including their neighborhoods, memories, and desires. Decisions about urban problems are often framed in rational, quantitative, and analytical terms of government bureaucracies with their valorization of speed (How quickly can I get from point A to point B?), capital (How much can the city gain in revenue from tourism?), and quantity (How many people are in Times Square at any given moment?). However, civic life is much more than that—it is a tearful 2 AM heartbreak on the corner of 7th Street and Avenue A; it is scrounging for quarters in between the cushions of your couch to make rent; and it is listening to wonderful (and, sometimes, horrible) musicians in the subway tunnels. What discussions of Smart Cities fail to account for is a holistic understanding of a full diversity of citizens that places value on their hopes, dreams, and aspirations. This speculative, future-oriented component removes the urgency of designing cities for today's problems with the notion of alternative possible futures based on more social, psychological, and emotional aspects that tend to be missing from discussions of urban technology.

A third motivation for the project was to explore the use of design methods such as visual prototypes, participatory design, and speculative design in order to extend and translate social science research beyond the academy. The use of visual prototypes is important as an alternative format for expressing complex socio-technical theories to a broader audience. For the most part, the work of social scientists is still measured by academic publications, which have a limited ability to circulate due to journal pricing, library access, and academic language barriers (across disciplines as well as between experts and practitioners). The use of participatory design introduces a different, more horizontal relationship between researchers and their field sites. As such, the researcher is no longer the expert who is studying the participants but rather the facilitator of (and also a participant in) a process. Both of these applications of design methods require a rethinking of traditional academic norms around research and publishing.

Value-Sensitive Design and Urban Technology

The role of socio-political values as embedded in urban technology (such as interfaces, street furniture, networked communication infrastructures, and personal technologies) has been an important site for research in media and communications, science and technology studies, urban planning, computer science, and human-computer interaction in the past ten years in tandem with the introduction of mobile phones, tablets, and laptops as well as the related software, systems, and networks. Scholars at the nexus of these fields have studied surveillance and security, privacy, intellectual property and open-source software, the digital divide and access to information, emergent forms of organizing (Humphreys, 2008), identity and sociality (Ito et al., 2005), as well as digital government and citizenship (Foth, 2008; Foth et al., 2011). For example, research on community wireless networks illustrated the ways in which bottom-up infrastructures introduced alternative possibilities for urban technology such as reduced cost, more widespread availability, and local ownership and control (Bar and Galperin, 2004, 2006; Sandvig, 2004, 2006; Sandvig et al., 2004; Meinrath, 2005; Bar and Park, 2006; Powell and Shade, 2006; Forlano, 2006, 2008; Forlano and Dailey, 2008; Powell, 2009; Forlano and Powell, 2011; Jungnickel, 2013). This project continues the focus on values in the still emergent, interdisciplinary field of urban informatics (Foth, 2008; Foth et al., 2011; Foth et al., 2011), which occupies space between some of the more traditional disciplines. One of the contributions of these studies has been to introduce new terminology that is useful in order to describe urban technology as well as emergent relationships between cities and socio-technical systems such as net locality (Gordon and Silva, 2011), code/space (Kitchin and Dodge, 2011), situated technologies (Shepard, 2011), and codescapes (Forlano, 2009).

This project draws on science and technology studies in order to emphasize the importance of understanding the ways in which socio-technical artifacts and infrastructures (Star, 1999) are imbued with socio-political values (Winner, 1986; Bijker et al., 1987; Nissenbaum, 2001) and invisible actors (Latour, 2005). In particular, the project uses a value sensitive design approach, which "accounts for human values, such as privacy, fairness, and democracy, throughout the design process" (Davis et al., 2006: 67). This approach considers the relationships between people and technologies as socio-technical systems in keeping with theories around the social construction of technology (Pinch and Bijker, 1984). Value-sensitive design emphasized the participation of direct and indirect stakeholders as well as multiple, iterative investigations to probe different aspects of a project. Value-sensitive design has been applied in a range of academic communities including human-computer interaction, computer-supported collaborative work, and information science (Friedman, 1996; Friedman and Nissenbaum, 1996; Nissenbaum, 2001; Le Dantec et al., 2009; Friedman et al., 2013).

In most cases, the design of digital technologies for cities does not consider the needs, goals, and values of citizens (Dourish and Bell, 2011). UrbanSim (Davis et al., 2006), Betaville (Skelton, 2013), and Hub2 (Gordon and Koo, 2008) are three examples of online platforms that allow participants to simulate and design their own cities and spaces with attention to their individual needs, values, desires, and goals. For example, Betaville is "a massively participatory online environment for distributed 3D design and development of proposals for changes to the built environment" that advocates for a "new form of open public design" (Skelton, 2013: online). Another interesting example is the Grow A Game project, which uses a value-sensitive design approach to redesign a traditional board game (Flanagan et al., 2005; Flanagan and Nissenbaum, 2007, 2014; Flanagan et al., 2007; Flanagan and Nissenbaum, 2008; Flanagan et al., 2008; Belman et al., 2011).

Many of these examples involve solution-oriented online platforms on which alternative urban spaces and cities can be designed around the values and needs of citizens. Our project differs from these in that it uses face-to-face participatory design workshops for the speculative and conceptual design of the technologies that mediate contemporary urban life such as urban screens, big data, the "Internet of things," and the quantified self.

Participatory Design Meets Speculative Design

In recent years, social scientists have become interested in working in modes that go beyond written text in academic journals. These include inventive methods (Lury and Wakeford, 2012) and public ethnography (Gans, 2010), as well as the creation of artifacts (Belman et al., 2011; Jungnickel, 2014), performances (Orr, 2006; Watts, 2012), exhibits (Latour and Weibel, 2005; Townsend et al., 2011), and constituencies through workshops and events (Loukissas et al., 2013; Greenspan et al., 2014). This project diverges from traditional social science methods and human-centered design methods in that it used a participatory design approach to structure a series of workshops. Between November 2012 and May 2013, three workshops were held, one each in Chicago, New York, and Boston. Each workshop was five hours in length and had approximately 30 participants, or five to six people per working group. Participants included a wide range of professions including designers, scholars, technologists, activists, policymakers, government leaders, businesspeople, and entrepreneurs. Rather than treating participants as research subjects, we understood them to be partners in a research process in line with recent thinking about moving beyond "designing for" and towards "designing with" (Schuler and Namioka, 1993; Winner, 1986; Sanders and Stappers, 2008).

We selected a codesign or participatory design (Kuhn and Winograd, 1996; Kensing and Blomberg, 1998; Sanders, 2002; Slocum, 2003; Muller, 2003; Spinuzzi, 2005; Sanders and Jan, 2008; Sanders and Westerlund, 2011) approach due to its history in the design of technology systems for workers in Scandinavia in the 1970s as well as its application in the field of Human-Computer Interaction more recently. In particular, participatory design is a useful approach for creating a format through which diverse stakeholders can share their ideas, become exposed to the ideas of others and generate new ideas. As a methodology, codesign is more active and hands-on than other methodologies that are common in public policy, such as town hall meetings and public hearings. Recent design scholarship explores the link between design—whether through objects, exhibits, or workshops—and the construction of publics and the building of political constituencies and publics around important policy issues (DiSalvo, 2009). In this project, we engaged a wide range of stakeholders in collaborative hands-on activities that have the potential to redefine meaningful citizen engagement. For example, citizens can be involved in placemaking, "citizen science," storytelling, or game play around important public policy issues. However, as many scholars have noted, participatory design should not be understood as a smooth or easy process for collaboration. In fact, the tensions and frictions that are likely to occur when diverse groups are convened may be one of the most valuable learnings from this methodology (Mouffe, 2003; Tsing, 2005; Hillgren et al., 2011). We can think of this as a kind of adversarial design (DiSalvo, 2012a), which is based on the theory of agonism in which there are potential benefits to political conflict. Finally, concepts such as things and infrastructuring (Björgvinsson et al., 2010) are helpful in understanding the ways in which participatory design can serve to raise conceptual questions and form constituencies and publics around important "matters of concern" (Latour and Weibel, 2005; DiSalvo, 2009; DiSalvo et al., 2011).

Furthermore, we were motivated by complementary design methodologies such as design fiction, speculative design, and critical design, which reach beyond identifying needs and solving problems, but rather, move towards a more generative, speculative, and future-oriented space of alternative possibilities (Dunne, 2001; Bleecker, 2009; DiSalvo, 2012b). While these methods, which were pioneered at Royal College of Art, have been criticized for their elitism because their work often does not move beyond the realm of the museum exhibit, we found value in bringing their future-orientation and ability to probe beyond everyday urban problems into conversation with participatory design. In particular, few disciplines are equipped to engage with future conditions and concerns to raise important questions about alternative possibilities and "what if" scenarios. In this project, we intentionally combined aspects of design fiction and speculative design with codesign and participatory design in order to take these design practices out of the context of art and museums and mobilized them as a generative practice for our participants.

Background

The codesign workshops were built on learnings from a number of previous codesign workshops by the co-authors. Specifically, in November 2011, the primary author ran a workshop on "Open Design for Organizational Innovation," which was funded by the National Science Foundation's Virtual Organizations as Sociotechnical Systems program and held at the St. Nicks Alliance in Brooklyn, New York in collaboration with Cornell University and Parsons The New School for Design. The purpose of the workshop, which was part of a series of workshops organized by the Design for Social Innovation and Sustainability (DESIS) Lab at Parsons The New School and funded by the Rockefeller Foundation's Cultural Innovation program, was to convene designers and social scientists around organizational challenges faced by the St. Nicks Alliance, a community development organization in North Brooklyn focused on issues such as housing, economic development, health, and children and families. The workshop included an ethnographic walking tour of the neighborhood in the morning in order to better understand the context, a presentation and discussion with the executive director of the St. Nicks Alliance, and a hands-on prototyping session in the afternoon.

Prior to this workshop, the primary author held a cosign workshop on "Measuring Social Impact" at the Center for Social Innovation, a coworking space in Toronto, as part of a 2011 Fulbright grant on "Networking Social Innovation in Urban Areas." In this case, the workshop participants were highly analytical, successful, and extremely time-pressed members of the coworking space who were activists and entrepreneurs committed to social change and environmental sustainability. In this workshop, some of the design methods that were introduced such as bodystorming (Schleicher et al., 2010), a kind of role playing exercise for brainstorming possible design futures, were perceived as not serious enough for the participants. However, after some discussion, the group decided to cluster their ideas for measuring social impact on a transparent wall using Post-It Notes. The clustering exercise allowed the group to take time to write down their individual ideas, organize their ideas along specific themes, and view the clusters. By the end of the workshop, participants seemed more open to the introduction of design methods in order to facilitate their discussion because they were able to see the value of the clustering exercise for quickly and relatively democratically honing in on important issues. In this case, the order of the activities may have been important; it might have been more successful to begin with a clustering exercise before moving into bodystorming or other design methods, which may seem intimidating and/or less analytical.

There was one previous project that served as a precedent to the Designing Policy codesign workshops in which the primary author convened multidisciplinary groups in experiential workshops, which is playfully referred to as "Flash Mob Ethnography," was initially part of the 2009 Breakout! Project, which was funded by The Architecture League of New York before being run in undergraduate and graduate courses, conferences, and workshops (Forlano, 2011). In this project, which was run in a range of spaces including urban neighborhoods, rural campuses, and high-end shopping malls, groups explored themes such as economic recession, community and belonging, and insiders and outsiders through hour-long ethnographic observations. The ethnographic observations were conducted by teams composed of designers and social scientists who were charged with taking notes and photos, making maps, and drawing sketches. Following the initial workshop which took place in Union Square in New York, participants collaboratively coded images from the ethnographic observation according to relevant themes and, finally, wrote a short collaborative article as part of a "writing sprint." These workshops explored peer production and collaborative research in the context of ethnographies of urban technology.

Alternative Urban Technology Futures: The Designing Policy Toolkit

In order to capture the theories, issues, and methodologies that we engaged with through this project, we produced a Designing Policy Toolkit. While the title suggests that we are "designing policy" itself, its intention is to communicate the ways in which urban technologies are in fact shaping the cities' politics and policies through their embedded value systems. The Designing Policy Toolkit is a large-format, visual communication poster that is folded into 12 double-sided panels. It is organized into three explanatory panels, which link a set of theoretical concerns and methodological approaches: urban technology, values in design, and codesign. On the back side, instructions about the codesign workshop format that was used in this project were presented. It is still available in hard copy by request and can be downloaded at http://designingpolicytoolkit.org.

The Designing Policy Toolkit is not a roadmap for how to create public policy as the name suggests, but rather it is a visual artifact that embodies an argument (Galey and Ruecker, 2010) and an approach for understanding the ways in which technologies embed socio-political values, thereby asserting power over our actions as citizens within urban environments. As a visual artifact, it is a prototype for an alternative publication and dissemination format that allows complex socio-technical concepts to become more legible and useful to practitioners and policymakers. Feminist scholars within science and technology studies have been advocating for alternative formats for the publication of scholarship and theory such as poetry, performance, and craft. In this way, a visual toolkit may be seen as an alternative to the journal article that acts as a device for the publication and circulation of ideas.

In the realm of public policy, there is some precedent for the use of more visual formats in order to convey complex information. For example, in 2003, the New America Foundation published the "Citizen's Guide to the Airwaves."[1] More recently, in 2001, the Institute for the Future published a 10-year forecast map, "A Planet of Civic Laboratories: The Future of Cities, Information, and Inclusion."[2] Finally, the Center for Urban Pedagogy's Making Policy Public has created a series of fold-out posters about issues including rent regulation and housing, immigration, transportation, and education.[3] Many of these artifacts are intended to convey complex scientific information in a straightforward way for the purpose of rendering it more legible to the general public. On the other hand, in recent years there has been renewed interest in media that offer instructions for do-it-yourself projects such as MAKE and Instructables, which explain a methodology, process, or approach.[4] In this vein, the Designing Policy Toolkit combines both an explanation of socio-technical expertise along with a methodology for bringing diverse stakeholders together.

The primary motivation for the creation of the toolkit was the translation of theories from science and technology studies and methodologies from design to the realm of public policy. Since the theories from science and technology studies are primarily published in academic journals, the toolkit can be understood as a boundary object (Star and Griesemer, 1989) that bridges multiple communities including scientific experts, policymakers, and amateurs. However, rather than being used by groups of individuals that are already affiliated with a particular organization or those that are already collaborating in a complex socio-technical domain, the toolkit is an invitation to examine the values embedded in the technologies that mediate a wide range of domains that are relevant in urban policymaking including education, healthcare, transportation, and housing.

As a designed artifact, however, the Designing Policy Toolkit is not without its own aesthetic politics (Rancière, 2010, 2013). For example, while developing the graphical style of the toolkit, we downloaded a series of illustrations from iStock's "Connected City" portfolio.[5] These images included illustrations of people, the built environment, transportation infrastructures, and telecommunications infrastructures, which were relevant for the representation of issues relevant to the toolkit. While we changed the color scheme, added our own features to the illustrations, and wrote the complementary text explaining the purpose and goals of the project, we were simultaneously—and, even, somewhat naively—appropriating the very look-and-feel of the Smart City, the connected city, and the techno-utopian city that we were attempting to challenge through the project. For example, we deliberately included users and non-users of technology, human and non-human actors (such as a group of multi-colored collaborative ants to signify diverse stakeholders working together), families, people riding buses and bicycles, and couples listening to music. These images were added specifically to introduce a multitude of activities that populate the urban domain rather than merely focusing on the use of technology. Furthermore, these images were intended to move discussions of technology away from a sole focus on privacy, transparency, and data access and towards a more holistic appreciation for urban life. For example, when presenting the project at a symposium, I instantly recognized that the imagery from one of the corporate Smart City projects was derived from the same set of illustrations that we had purchased from iPhoto. Such are the politics embedded within image databases, which have a way of seeping into visual work. Thus, by using commercial images of connected cities, we revealed the risk of inadvertently promoting a contradictory set of politics. In sum, the toolkit illustrates a need for greater attention to the politics of aesthetic choices in future visual work.

The Designing Policy toolkit was sent electronically to all of the participants in the codesign workshops and, when requested, it was sent out in hard copy as well. As a visual communication piece that captures a set of theoretical and methodological research interests, it serves as a tangible artifact that can bridge a conversation between experts and amateurs as well as across disciplines. In some ways, while the toolkit is a complex explanatory artifact that brings together diverse perspectives, at the same time, like other artifacts produced as design fictions and scenarios about emerging technologies, it lacks a sense of the tensions, conflicts, frictions, frustrations, and difficulties present within cities (Mouffe, 2003; Tsing, 2005; Hillgren et al., 2011). Where are the homeless people and other so-called "undesirables" (Whyte, 2000)? Where are the honking horns, traffic jams, and bicycle accidents? Where are the everyday rage-filled interactions and unexplainable acts of kindness that fill our streets, parks, and public spaces in contemporary urban life?

Overall, reactions to the Designing Policy Toolkit have been enthusiastic and supportive among scholars, policymakers, technologists, and design practitioners. For example, in May 2014, the City of Boston's Office of New Urban Mechanics requested 20 copies. While it is too early to understand the ways in which the toolkit functioned in terms of translating theoretical concepts and methodological approaches, as a working prototype, it offers a glimpse of the potential for creating visual artifacts that represent complex socio-technical issues and approaches for the purpose of translation to a wider community around urban technology.

Engaging Stakeholders in Building Urban Technology: Designing Policy Workshops

In the Designing Policy project, we built on this previous workshop experience, by holding a series of three multi-stakeholder codesign workshops on urban communication and urban informatics in Chicago, New York, and Boston between November 2012 and May 2013. Each workshop was five hours in length and had approximately 30 participants, or five to six people per working group. The workshops used open and participatory design methods to engage approximately 30 local policymakers, entrepreneurs, activists, academics, graduate students, and citizens in discussions and hands-on activities that allowed us to reimagine the ways in which digital technologies can be embedded in public spaces for the purposes of citizen engagement.

The workshops explored the possibilities, affordances, and constraints of a different digital technology platform (interfaces, artifacts, infrastructures), mode of citizen engagement (placemaking, "citizen science," storytelling) and set of values (openness and transparency, sustainability and resilience). In particular, the digital technology platforms that were workshops include interfaces such as urban screens, mobile applications, and web sites; artifacts such as physical hardware and the "internet of things" (Kuniavsky, 2010); and, infrastructures such as low-power wireless devices such as radio frequency identification tags (RFIDs), sensors, QR codes, and Wi-Fi routers and networks.

The first workshop focused on the deployment and use of interactive urban screens for cultural, social, and political engagement in policy issues in Chicago. This was based on an earlier project by the second author in which, in Spring 2012, graduate students in his Interactive Media workshop created a set of placemaking prototypes for the City of Chicago's 2012 Cultural Plan, which were deployed at City Hall, the National Museum of Mexican Art, and the Old Town School of Folk Music. The second workshop explored the use of the "internet of things" in post-crisis New York; considering the impact of environmental crises such as Superstorm Sandy as well as financial crises such as the economic recession that began in 2008. With respect to environmental crises, digital platforms such as Pachube.com have been used to allow citizens to participate in "citizen science." This topic built on the first author's Spring 2012 Networked Objects workshop in which graduate students worked on projects that engaged mobile and mesh networking technologies with grassroots partner organizations. Specifically, one project focused the use of mobile technologies to coordinate an urban farming initiative in partnership with Toronto-based non-profit Not Far From the Tree and another focused on developing applications specifically for integration with community-owned mesh networks in partnership with the New America Foundation. Finally, the third workshop explored technologies of the body and health in Boston due to the city's well-known health infrastructure.

The workshops were documented in photos (over 100 photos were taken during each workshop) and, occasionally, by video (video documentation was taken only during the initial workshop in Chicago). In addition, following the first workshop, the co-authors met with the five facilitators who were graduate students from the Institute of Design at Illinois Institute of Technology in order to better understand what elements of the workshop worked well and what aspects needed to be changed for the subsequent workshops in New York and Boston. The initial results of the workshops are described below. There were no formal interviews or surveys conducted with workshop participants since the focus was on framing the workshops as an open learning activity rather than participation in a research experiment or study.

Following initial introductions, ice-breakers, and a brief presentation about the specific urban technology topic of the workshop (urban screens, "internet of things," technologies of the body), the majority of the workshop was focused on hands-on exercises in which groups moved through various stages of a design process from brainstorming to prototyping and presenting to critique. Design artifacts such as large-scale tabletop sheets with space for notes and sketches, colorful cards with values, and design methods cards were helpful for structuring the workshops with the support of facilitators who guided participants through the activities.

1. *Contextualizing the Discussion in a Specific Neighborhood* (20 minutes): First, we invited people to discuss the neighborhood where they live in order to contextualize the discussion in the lived experience of the city. Next, we asked each group to choose a neighborhood to focus the discussion on designing for a specific community. Finally, we asked groups to draw a map (geographical or metaphorical) of the neighborhood, pointing out the important sites of community interaction such as where people typically hang out.
2. *Developing a Shared Understanding of Values* (20 minutes): First, each group was assigned a value card, which was placed on the table. It is important to note that we deliberately avoided the common values that are typically associated with urban technology such as privacy and security or efficiency and innovation. Instead, we substituted a list of values that we thought would provide for a more generative and critical discussion. These were: romantic, serenity, telepathy, serendipity, creativity, borderlessness, and invisible. Next, we asked each group to discuss what the value meant to them and asked them to tell a personal story about the value. Finally, we asked them to discuss the ways in which they might embed the value (or their group's reframing of it) into their city.
3. *Brainstorming and Prototyping* (2 hours): In this section, participants used a design fiction (Bleecker, 2009; Dunne and Raby, 2013) approach by orienting their discussions towards designing for a future city scenario, at least 25–30 years in the future. The purpose of this future orientation was to remove the limitations and constraints of our everyday lived experiences in order to encourage creativity and openness to new ideas that, while not feasible today, may rely on a near-future technology, capability, or situation.

First, each group brainstormed projects, platforms, and services that respond to and build on the ideas around values that they explored in the previous discussion. In this section, the focus was on coming up with as many ideas as possible without judging their feasibility and making these ideas tangible and visible through sketches, notes, and diagrams. Next, groups were asked to choose one of their ideas to prototype and select the format in which they would represent their prototype. These formats included interactive scenarios, multi-layered maps, and Lego models. Through the creation of the prototype, groups were forced to bring their ideas to life as they thought through the complex opportunities and tradeoffs embedded within their ideas.

4. *Presenting and Critique* (1 hour): At the end of the workshop, groups were asked to present their prototypes by acting out or describing their process and ideas. Workshop participants were asked to take part in a "design critique" style conversation in which they could provide feedback about the prototypes. The purpose of the critique was not to criticize but rather to help the project move forward towards a shared goal. Participants were guided to begin their critique with positive feedback, next discuss limitations and, finally, end with alternatives and proposals in order to move the project forward.

Design Frictions in Participatory Design

This paper mobilizes the notion of frictions, controversies, and dilemmas that have been developed in recent design scholarship. Building on Chantal Mouffe's work on "agonistic spaces" (2003), Hillgren et al. (2011) state:

> "Another related perspective is to consider prototypes as vehicles able to raise questions as well as highlight controversies and dilemmas. The importance of allowing controversies to exist side by side, instead of negotiating them into consensus ... " (174)

In the following section, we will discuss a range of examples of frictions and tensions that we observed through engagement with the workshop participants and consider the ways in which they might be used for infrastructuring (Björgvinsson et al., 2010) in order to form constituencies (DiSalvo, 2009) around important "matters of concern" (Latour and Weibel, 2005).

One of these tensions is around the embedded values in some of the examples of urban technology that we showed in order to initiate the conversation. For example, at the first workshop in Chicago, which focused on urban screens and culture, we offered a wide range of artistic and commercial examples including the latest examples of urban advertising. One particular example, was Axe's "Even Angels Will Fall" men's deodorant campaign in which scantily clad women with wings appeared to fall into public squares using digital projection. However, we did not specifically spend a lot time to discuss the embedded values in these examples following the presentation since the values discussion was part of the later section of the workshop. While we assumed that the topic of embedded values was clear in our initial framing of the workshop, we found that this topic exposed a tension around gender and, in particular, feminist technology perspectives (Haraway, 1991). However, since one of the group facilitators was able to raise her criticism of this particular example of urban advertising, it became an important component in the discussion of gender as it is built into urban spaces and infrastructures. As the group moved from discussing a particular Chicago neighborhood to discussing values, they were able to reframe the "value card" that we had given them from "telepathy" to "tel-empathy" as a means of illustrating the way in which citizens might engage with the city in a more empathic way. Through prototyping with multi-layered maps, the group was able to create an idea for a wayfinding platform that allowed citizens to explore different neighborhoods for the purpose of greater understanding.

A second tension related to the embedded values in the values that we selected as focal points for the workshop. We deliberately wanted to move away from discussions of the top-down logics of efficiency, security, and innovation as well as the more bottom-up advocacy for transparency, privacy, and engagement. Instead, we wanted to move into a more playful but still rigorous discussion about how we might design alternative sets of values in order to open the "black box" of urban technologies. However, we found that, in some ways, the values that we selected reproduced some of the common debates around urban technology and ubiquitous computing. We were inspired by Italo Calvino's *Invisible Cities* (2010) as well as Georg Simmel's 1903 "The Metropolis and Mental Life" (2002), which feared that urbanization would have a negative impact on individual psychology since we would no longer have a sense of community. Yet, in selecting values such as borderlessness, invisibility, and serendipity, we reinforced some of the revolutionary claims of technology evangelists that we have long fought to overturn in other scholarship (Forlano, 2013). For example, Mark Weiser's (1991) manifesto on ubiquitous computing that advocated for the creation of many invisible computers, which has been discussed by Dourish and Bell (2011). While the purpose of the codesign activity was for participants to reframe the specific value that their group had been assigned in line with their own lived experiences, this intention did not always translate clearly. Rather by selecting a set of values to inspire the prototyping activity, we were forced to re-examine our own understandings and values.

A third tension relates to our focus on urban technology as the site for reimagining alternative possible futures. While social scientists are often satisfied with descriptions of existing realities and lived experiences, designers are engaged in asking "what if" and generating responses to existing and imagined possibilities. Our belief in the possibility of posing questions that open the "black box" of urban technology as a site for politics as well as our interest in spurring conversation on building city systems that better reflect the everyday lives of citizens led us to focus the workshops specifically on urban technology. However, this framing as tied specifically to advancing certain kinds of urban technologies, could be understood, in some ways, as techno-deterministic in that it seems to assume that there are technological solutions to urban problems. At the same time, we understand technology to be socio-technical and have a very broad view of what might constitute a technology. For example, rather than limited to specific devices and platforms, urban technologies might include the built environment and public spaces, and transportation and communications systems, as well as social systems and forms of organizing. For participants who rejected this framing outright, this was a point of contention, which sometimes made it difficult to move forward into the prototyping activity. Yet, we believe that the workshops fulfilled the objective of opening up a space for a range of perspectives around technology—whether techno-utopian or dystopian, techno-deterministic, or socially constructed—to be discussed and confronted. This illustrates the nature of what it means to have a materially-engaged critical urban technology practice that can generate new questions, framings and concepts that open the "black box" without being overly techno-deterministic.

The fourth friction relates to the difference between modes of engagement and ways of working that we designed into the prototyping activity and those that were familiar to our participants. For example, our goal was to engage policymakers in values-based discussions of urban technology. While we invited many policymakers including city council members and city aldermen, and received positive responses and intentions to participate in the workshop, the deadline oriented nature of their work precluded many from attending. In one instance, during the prototyping activity, a city alderman took a leadership role in helping the group to better understand some of the issues and challenges faced in her district. At first, while building a Lego model of her neighborhood intersection, she instructed various group members to add specific components of the model, playing the role of a kind of construction foreman for the team. However, as the model became more elaborate and exciting, she also became more activity engaged by jumping in to help build the model. In contrast, another group sat in a circular discussion throughout the prototyping session but did not manage to create or build anything. This verified our belief that material engagement with the ideas through prototyping was helpful and even necessary in order to move the ideas forward and collaboratively build on the ideas. Some of the examples of the prototypes that were created in order to engage in these complex socio-technical conversations included multi-layer maps with location-based tours of specific city neighborhoods in Chicago, emotionally aware balloons that floated through a neighborhood in Cambridge, Lego models with interactive street furniture and physical "on-ramps to the Internet" in New York, and elaborate interactive scenarios about surveillance and citizen activism that were acted out with signs and props.

The last tension that we exposed through engaging with multiple stakeholders using participatory design was the shift from designer as expert or design researcher to designer as facilitator or change-maker. For example, in human-centered design, designers conduct research for the purpose of informing or inspiring their design process. Similarly, in social science, it is common to conduct interviews and observations for the purpose of building knowledge or theory. However, there is no particular imperative to return to the "users," "informants," or field once the research has been completed. In addition, this hierarchical relationship is codified through university institutional review board (IRB) approvals and consent forms that aim to protect human subjects but, at the same time, treat them as "subjects" of research rather than partners in a learning process. For this reason, while we used best practices in research ethics such as informing workshop participants that this was a research project and that we would be documenting it through notes, photos, and videos, we deliberately designed the workshop around the understanding that participants are experts on their own experiences; for example, on living and working in particular neighborhoods of a city. Yet, despite attempting to create an environment around collaboration, we found that some participants still mistrust the premises of such workshops because of prior experiences with researchers and/or universities that pursue their own goals such as publications and grants without consideration of the situations, needs, and goals of their so-called subjects. For this reason, IRB guidelines should be reviewed with participatory design and other collaborative practices in mind so that regulations do not impose unnecessary hierarchies among researchers and participants. This might include rethinking consent forms as more of a "memorandum of understanding" and allowing for increased data sharing (especially related to photos, videos, and notes) rather than imposing some of the standard boilerplate language that is often used to secure data.

Future Implications

Building on the learnings from these workshops, the primary author of this paper has co-organized a number of subsequent codesign workshops focused on different issues such as natural resources, urban health, and the future of work including:

- "Experiments in (and out of) the Studio: Art and Design Methods for Science and Technology Studies," which was held at Copenhagen Business School in Copenhagen, Denmark in October 2012 and funded by Goldsmiths University and Microsoft Research;
- "digitalSTS and Design Workshop," which was held at Harvard University's Arnold Arboretum in Boston, MA in June 2013; and,

- "Reimagining Work," which was held at the Institute of Design at Illinois Institute of Technology in September 2014 and funded by the Open Society Foundations.

These subsequent workshops have allowed for the continued iteration and testing of the codesign principles including the values of prototyping as introduced in the Designing Policy Toolkit. Future publications will explore the issues, formats, and methods that have been used in these subsequent workshops. However, we believe that codesign methods have great potential for application in the field of urban technology and beyond as a means of building constituencies and publics around important policy issues.

Conclusion

One of the most valuable lessons of this project, which focused on discussions of embedded values in urban technology such as urban screens, the "internet of things," and quantified self, was to reveal our own biases and values through engagement with codesign methods at workshops in three major metropolitan centers of the United States—Chicago, New York, and Boston. The workshops engaged a wide range of stakeholders—from policymakers and entrepreneurs to activists and academics—in hands-on activities about urban technology. In contrast to studies that focus on the use of codesign for consensus-building, this paper introduces the term design friction to capture a range of examples of the ways in which tension, conflict, or disagreement allowed for the discussion of urban technology to move out of the "black box" and into prototyping alternative possible futures and questions rather than problem solving for today's challenges. The result of the workshops was a visual codesign toolkit, which was developed in order to demonstrate the ways in which urban technologies are embedded with values as well as to illustrate how codesign methods can enable diverse stakeholders to come together around complex socio-technical questions that are shaping everyday life in cities.

In engaging participants in conversations about the role of values in urban technology, we learned the ways in which codesign might be used to create constituencies and publics around important "matters of concern." At the same time, we uncovered the ways in which values were embedded in everything from the selection of graphic icons for the toolkit, the framing of the workshops around technology and the gendered nature of some of the commercial examples of urban technology. Ultimately, the tensions between our own understandings and assumptions and those of our participants were productive in that they allowed people to explore complex socio-technical issues through material engagement in prototyping in order to raise important questions about the values and biases present in urban technology.

Notes

1. See <http://www.wirelessfuture.newamerica.net/publications/policy/citizens_guide_to_the_airwaves>. Accessed on July 9, 2014.
2. See <http://www.iftf.org/our-work/global-landscape/human-settlement/the-future-of-cities-information-and-inclusion/>. Accessed July 9, 2014.
3. See <http://www.welcometocup.org/Store?program_id=1>. Accessed July 9, 2014.

4. See <http://www.instructables.com>. Accessed July 9, 2014.
5. See <http://www.istockphoto.com/vector/connected-city-27031404>. Accessed July 9, 2014.

Acknowledgments

We would like to thank the Urban Communication Foundation for their support of this research as well as all of the participants and facilitators who contributed to the workshops. In addition, we would like to acknowledge the Institute of Design at Illinois Institute of Technology, the Center for Social Innovation and Emerson College for providing venues for the workshops.

Bibliography

F. Bar and H. Galperin, "Building the Wireless Internet Infrastructure: From Cordless Ethernet Archipelagos to Wireless Grids," *Communications and Strategies* 54: 2 (2004) 45–68.

F. Bar and H. Galperin, "Geeks, Cowboys, and Bureaucrats: Deploying Broadband, the Wireless Way," *The Southern African Journal of Information and Communication (SAJIC)* 6 (2006) 48–63.

F. Bar and N. Park, "Municipal Wi-Fi Networks: The Goals, Practices, and Policy Implications of the U. S. Case," *Communications & Stratégies* 61 (2006) 107–125.

J. Belman, M. Flanagan, H. Nissenbaum, and J. Diamond, "Grow-A-Game: A Tool for Values Conscious Design and Analysis of Digital Games," paper presented at the Proceedings of DiGRA 2011 Conference: Think Design Play (Hilversum, The Netherlands, 2011).

W.E. Bijker, T.P. Hughes, and T. Pinch, *The Social Construction of Technological Systems* (Cambridge, MA: The MIT Press, 1987).

E. Björgvinsson, P. Ehn, and P.-A. Hillgren, "Participatory Design and Democratizing Innovation," paper presented at the Proceedings of the 11th Biennial Participatory Design Conference (2010).

J. Bleecker, "Design Fiction: A Short Essay on Design, Science, Fact and Fiction" (2009) <http://www.nearfuturelaboratory.com/2009/03/17/design-fiction-a-short-essay-on-design-science-fact-and-fiction/>.

I. Calvino, *Invisible Cities* (New York: Random House, 2010).

J. Davis, P. Lin, A. Borning, B. Friedman, P.H. Kahn, and P.A. Waddell, "Simulations for Urban Planning: Designing for Human Values," *Computer* 39: 9 (2006) 66–72.

C. DiSalvo, "Design and the Construction of Publics," *Design Issues* 25: 1 (2009) 48–63.

C. DiSalvo, *Adversarial Design* (Cambridge, MA: MIT Press, 2012a).

C. DiSalvo, "Spectacles and Tropes: Speculative Design and Contemporary Food Cultures," *The Fibreculture Journal* 20 (2012b) 109–122.

C. DiSalvo, T. Lodato, L. Fries, B. Schechter, and T. Barnwell, "The Collective Articulation of Issues as Design Practice," *CoDesign* 7: 3–4 (2011) 185–197.

P. Dourish and G. Bell, *Divining a Digital Future: Mess and Mythology in Ubiquitous Computing* (Cambridge, MA: MIT Press, 2011).

A. Dunne, *Hertzian Tales: Electronic Products, Aesthetic Experience, and Critical Design* (Cambridge, MA: MIT Press, 2001).

A. Dunne and F. Raby, *Speculative Everything: Design, Fiction, and Social Dreaming* (Cambridge, MA: MIT Press, 2013).

M. Flanagan and H. Nissenbaum, "A Game Design Methodology to Incorporate Social Activist Themes," paper presented at the Proceedings of the SIGCHI conference on Human factors in computing systems (2007).

M. Flanagan and H. Nissenbaum, "Design Heuristics for Activist Games," in C. Heeter and Y. Kafai, eds., *Beyond Barbie to Mortal Kombat* (Cambridge: MIT Press, 2008) 265–280.

M. Flanagan and H. Nissenbaum, *Values at Play in Digital Games* (Cambridge, MA: MIT Press, 2014).

M. Flanagan, D.C. Howe, and H. Nissenbaum, "Values at Play: Design Tradeoffs in Socially-oriented Game Design," paper presented at the Proceedings of the SIGCHI conference on Human factors in computing systems (2005).

M. Flanagan, H. Nissenbaum, J. Belman, and J. Diamond, "A Method for Discovering Values in Digital Games," paper presented at the Situated Play, Proceedings of DiGRA 2007 Conference (2007).

M. Flanagan, D. Howe, and H. Nissenbaum, "Embodying Values in Technology: Theory and Practice," *Information Technology and Moral Philosophy* (2008) 322–353.

L. Forlano, "Activist Infrastructures: The Role of Community Wireless Organizations in Authenticating the City," *Eastbound* 1 (2006) 50–66.

L. Forlano, "Anytime? Anywhere?: Reframing Debates Around Community and Municipal Wireless Networking," *Journal of Community Informatics* 4: 1 (2008).

L. Forlano, "WiFi Geographies: When Code Meets Place," *The Information Society* 25 (2009) 344–352.

L. Forlano, "Building the Open Source City: New Work Environments for Collaboration and Innovation," in L. Forlano, M. Foth, C. Satchell and M. Gibbs, eds., *From Social Butterfly to Engaged Citizen* (Cambridge, MA: MIT Press, 2011) 437–460.

L. Forlano, "Making Waves: Urban Technology and the Coproduction of Place," *First Monday* 18: 11 (2013).

L. Forlano and D. Dailey, *Community Wireless Networks as Situated Advocacy* (New York, NY: The Architecture League of New York, 2008).

L. Forlano and A. Powell, *From the Digital Divide to Digital Excellence: Global Best Practices for Municipal and Community Wireless Networks* (Washington, D.C. New America Foundation, 2011).

M. Foth, *Handbook of Research on Urban Informatics: The Practice and Promise of the Real-Time City* (Hershey, PA: IGI Global, 2008).

M. Foth, J.H.-j. Choi, and C. Satchell, "Urban Informatics," paper presented at the Computer Supported Collaborative Work (Hangzhou, China, 2011).

M. Foth, L. Forlano, M. Gibbs, and C. Satchell, *From Social Butterfly to Engaged Citizen: Urban Informatics, Social Media, Ubiquitous Computing, and Mobile Technology to Support Citizen Engagement* (Cambridge, MA: MIT Press, 2011).

B. Friedman, "Value-sensitive Design," *Interactions* 3: 6 (1996) 16–23.

B. Friedman and H. Nissenbaum, "Bias in Computer Systems," *ACM Transactions on Information Systems (TOIS)* 14: 3 (1996) 330–347.

B. Friedman, P.H. Kahn Jr, A. Borning, and A. Huldtgren, "Value Sensitive Design and Information Systems" *Early Engagement and New Technologies: Opening Up the Laboratory* (Springer, 2013) 55–95.

A. Galey and S. Ruecker, "How a Prototype Argues," *Literary and Linguistic Computing* 25: 4 (2010) 405–424.

H.J. Gans, "Public Ethnography; Ethnography as Public Sociology," *Qualitative Sociology* 33: 1 (2010) 97–104.

E. Gordon and G. Koo, "Placeworlds: Using Virtual Worlds to Foster Civic Engagement," *Space and Culture* 11: 3 (2008) 204–221.

E. Gordon and A.de.S.e. Silva, *Net Locality: Why Location Matters in a Networked World* (Chichester, West Sussex; Malden, MA: Wiley-Blackwell, 2011).

A. Greenfield, "Against the Smart City (The City is here for you to Use)," *Do Projects, New York City* (2013).

A. Greenspan, S. Lindtner, and D. Li, Hacked Matter (2014) <http://www.hackedmatter.com> Accessed June 12, 2014.

D.J. Haraway, "A Cyborg Manifesto: Science, Technology, and Socialist-feminism in the Late Twentieth Century," *Simians, Cyborgs and Women: The Reinvention of Nature* (1991) 149–181.

P.-A. Hillgren, A. Seravalli, and A. Emilson, "Prototyping and Infrastructuring in Design for Social Innovation," *CoDesign* 7: 3–4 (2011) 169–183.

Humphreys, "Mobile Social Networks and Social Practice: A Case Study of Dodgeball," *Journal of Computer-Mediated Communication* 13: 1 (2008) 341–360.

M. Ito, D. Okabe, and M. Matsuda, *Personal, Portable, Pedestrian: Mobile Phones in Japanese Life* (Cambridge, MA: MIT Press, 2005).

K. Jungnickel, *DiY WiFi: Re-imagining Connectivity* (London: Palgrave, 2013).

K. Jungnickel, *Bikes and Bloomers* (2014) <http://bikesandbloomers.com> Accessed June 12, 2014.

F. Kensing and J. Blomberg, "Participatory Design: Issues and Concerns," *Computer Supported Cooperative Work (CSCW)* 7: 3–4 (1998) 167–185.

R. Kitchin and M. Dodge, *Code/space: Software and Everyday Life* (Cambridge, MA: MIT Press, 2011).

S. Kuhn and T. Winograd, "Profile: Participatory Design," in T. Winograd, ed., *Bringing Design to Software* (New York, NY: ACM Press, 1996), 290–294.

M. Kuniavsky, *Smart Things: Ubiquitous Computing User Experience Design* (Amsterdam; Boston: Morgan Kaufmann Publisher, 2010).

B. Latour, *Reassembling the Social: an Introduction to Actor-network-theory* (Oxford: Oxford University Press, 2005).

B. Latour and P. Weibel, *Making Things Public: Atmospheres of Democracy* (Cambridge, MA: MIT Press, 2005).

C.A. Le Dantec, E.S. Poole, and S.P. Wyche, "Values as Lived Experience: Evolving Value Sensitive Design in Support of Value Discovery," paper presented at the Proceedings of the SIGCHI conference on human factors in computing systems (2009).

Y. Loukissas, L. Forlano, D. Ribes, and J. Vertesi, *digitalSTS and Design* (2013) <http://stsdesignworkshop.tumblr.com> Accessed June 12, 2014.

C. Lury and N. Wakeford, *Inventive Methods: The Happening of the Social* (New York: Routledge, 2012).

S. Meinrath, "Community Wireless Networking and Open Spectrum Usage: A Research Agenda to Support Progressive Policy Reform of the Public Airwaves," *The Journal of Community Informatics* 1: 2 (2005) 174–179.

C. Mouffe, "Pluralism, Dissensus and Democratic Citizenship," *II Seminário internacional educação intercultural, gênero e movimentos sociais. Identidade, diferença, mediações* (2003) 1–10.

M.J. Muller, "Participatory Design: the Third Space in HCI," *Human-computer Interaction: Development Process* (2003) 165–185.

H. Nissenbaum, "How Computer Systems Embody Values," *Computer* 34: 3 (2001) 117–119.

J. Orr, *Panic Diaries: a Genealogy of Panic Disorder* (Durham, NC: Duke University Press, 2006).

T.J. Pinch and W.E. Bijker, "The Social Construction of Facts and Artefacts: Or How the Sociology of Science and the Sociology of Technology Might Benefit Each Other," *Social Studies of Science* 14: 3 (1984) 399–441.

A. Powell, "WiFi Publics: Producing Community and Technology," *Information, Communication & Society* 11: 8 (2009) 1068–1088. December 2008.

A. Powell and L.R. Shade, "Going Wi-Fi in Canada: Municipal and Community Initiatives," *Government Information Quarterly* 23: 3–4 (2006) 381–403.

J. Rancière, *Dissensus: On Politics and Aesthetics* (New York: Bloomsbury Publishing, 2010).

J. Rancière, *The Politics of Aesthetics* (London: A&C Black, 2013).

E.B.-N. Sanders, "From User-centered to Participatory Design Approaches," *Design and the Social Sciences: Making Connections* (2002) 1–8.

E.B.-N. Sanders and P.J. Stappers, "Co-Creation and the New Landscapes of Design," *CoDesign* 4: 1 (2008) 5–18.

E.B.-N. Sanders and B. Westerlund, "Experiencing, Exploring and Experimenting in and with Co-design Spaces," *Nordes* 4 (2011) 1–5.

C. Sandvig, "An Initial Assessment of Cooperative Action in Wi-Fi Networking," *Telecommunications Policy*, 28: 7/8 (2004) 579–602.

C. Sandvig, "Disorderly Infrastructure and the Role of Government," *Government Information Quarterly* 23: 3–4 (2006) 503–506.

C. Sandvig, D. Young, and S. Meinrath, "Hidden Interfaces to 'Ownerless' Networks," paper presented at the 32nd Conference on Communication, Information, and Internet Policy (Washington, DC, 2004).

D. Schleicher, P. Jones, and O. Kachur, "Bodystorming as Embodied Designing," *Interactions* (Nov.–Dec.) (2010).

D. Schuler and A. Namioka, *Participatory Design: Principles and Practices* (Hillsdale, N.J. L. Erlbaum Associates, 1993).

M. Shepard, ed., *Sentient City: Ubiquitous Computing, Architecture, and the Future of Urban Space* (Cambridge, MA: MIT Press, 2011).

G. Simmel, "The Metropolis and Mental Life (1903)," in G. Bridge and S. Watson, eds, *The Blackwell City Reader* (Oxford and Malden, MA: Wiley-Blackwell, 2002).

C. Skelton, *Soft City Culture and Technology: The Betaville Project* (New York: Springer Publishing Company, Incorporated, 2013).

N. Slocum, "Participatory Methods Toolkit: A Practitioner's Manual," *ViWTA and King Baudoin Foundation* (2003).

C. Spinuzzi, "The Methodology of Participatory Design," *Technical Communication* 52: 2 (2005) 163–174.

S.L. Star, "The Ethnography of Infrastructure," *American Behavioral Scientist* 43: 3 (1999) 377.

S.L. Star and J.R. Griesemer, "Institutional Ecology, Translations' and Boundary Objects: Amateurs and Professionals in Berkeley's Museum of Vertebrate Zoology, 1907–39," *Social Studies of Science* 19: 3 (1989) 387–420.

A. Townsend, *Smart Cities: Big Data, Civic Hackers, and the Quest for a New Utopia* (New York, NY: W. W. Norton & Company, 2013).

A. Townsend, L. Forlano, and A. Simeti, "Breakout! Escape from the Office: Situating Knowledge Work in Sentient Public Spaces," in M. Shepard, ed., *Sentient City* (Cambridge, MA: MIT Press, 2011).

A.L. Tsing, *Friction: An Ethnography of Global Connection* (Princeton, NJ: Princeton University Press, 2005).

L. Watts, The Design Mailboat (2012) <http://www.sand14.com/?p=277> Accessed June 12, 2014.

M. Weiser, "The Computer for the 21st Century," *Scientific American* 265: 3 (1991) 94–104.

W.H. Whyte, *The Social Life of Small Urban Spaces* (Washington, DC: The Conservation Foundation, 2000).

L. Winner, "Do Artifacts Have Politics?," in L. Winner, ed., *The Whale and the Reactor: A Search for Limits in an Age of High Technology* (Chicago: University of Chicago Press, 1986).

Technology-Enabled Participatory Platforms for Civic Engagement: The Case of U.S. Cities

Kevin C. Desouza and Akshay Bhagwatwar

ABSTRACT *Technology-enabled participatory platforms are proving to be valuable canvases for engaging citizens in solving public-good challenges. Citizens are playing a more active role by either designing platforms themselves or participating on platforms created by public agencies. Unfortunately, our theoretical knowledge about the nature of these platforms is limited. In this paper, we take the first steps towards understanding technology-enabled participatory platforms. Through an exploratory analysis, following the spirit of a grounded theoretic methodology, we examined technology-enabled participatory platforms in the 25 most populated cities in the United States. We deduce four main archetypes*—citizen centric and citizen data, citizen centric and government data, government centric and citizen data, *and* government centric and citizen-developed solutions *of technology-enabled participatory platforms. We describe the intricacies of how collective intelligence is leveraged on these platforms. Implications for local government managers and urban planners are discussed. We hypothesize how the future of these platforms might evolve in the not so distant future.*

Introduction

> *We must not innovate for citizens, we must innovate with citizens ... We have to create canvases for citizens to collaborate to tackle challenges and advance their communities ... Exploiting technology is central to the goal of designing future civic-engagement platforms – A City Manager*

Civic engagement continues to be a salient concept in the public administration, public policy, governance, and urban planning literatures (see, e.g., Bimber, 2000; Jennings and Zeitner, 2003; Tolbert and McNeal, 2003). Traditionally, public agencies have taken the lead in designing platforms for civic engagement and participation (e.g., consider traditional town hall meetings). The barriers to participation are non-trivial (e.g., taking time off work or having to travel to city hall for hearings on an issue). In addition, the traditional modes for sourcing input on civic matters have limitations when operating with large and diverse populations. Due to advancements in information and communication technologies (ICTs), we have seen the emergence of technology-enabled participatory platforms for civic engagement in the last few years (Desouza, 2012a).

Technology-enabled participatory platforms can be defined as forums created to source, analyze, visualize, and share information, expertise, and solutions to advance social causes and/or solve social and policy problems. These platforms not only address some traditional concerns about civic engagement—such as lowering the barriers for citizens to engage—but have also promoted a wave of innovation around how citizens tackle local challenges and realize opportunities collectively. Consider the example of Textizen (www.textizen.com), a mobile and web-based platform that allows public agencies and citizens to interact regarding local issues. The platform is currently available in multiple cities including Philadelphia, Salt Lake City, Chicago, Tampa, Oakland, and Portland. The platform enables conversations between public agencies and citizens in the form of a question-answer discussion. The platform offers an interface where the public agencies or citizens can post a survey or a single question regarding a local issue. Users of the platform get notified about a new survey/question through their mobile application. In addition, the public agencies also use flyers to raise awareness and direct citizens to the application or to a number to which they can text their response. Citizens can also create conversations centered on the local issue, which could potentially lead to more questions that seek citizen responses. The platform has a dashboard through which user responses to particular surveys/questions are visible, thus helping public agencies understand citizen opinion on issues. Textizen acts as a replacement for traditional offline mechanisms of civic engagement such as town hall meetings or mail-based surveys. Technology-enabled participatory platforms such as Textizen play a vital role in civic engagement and mobilization.

In recent years, the notion of crowdfunding and crowdsourcing—where citizens get together, gather the available resources, and resolve local issues that matter to them—has also gained importance (Dirks and Keeling, 2009). An example of a crowdsourcing initiative is the Santa Cruz budget shortfall resolution. In 2009, the City of Santa Cruz in California faced a budget shortfall of $9.2 million dollars. To find a potential resolution to the problem, the city asked its residents for help. The general population helped the city analyze its financial records, generated many new ideas to resolve the shortfall, and then used an online platform to discern the strongest ideas by voting. With the help of less than 10 percent of its population, the city was able to create solutions that resolved the budget shortfall. This example highlights how crowdsourcing and crowdfunding initiatives enable public agencies to work outside the traditional, or established, structures and engage citizens in innovative ways such that local issues are resolved without causing much strain on their resources.

The increased interest in technology-enabled civic engagement platforms and bottom-up organizing models such as crowdsourcing and crowdfunding has created an opportunity to transform the dynamics of citizen engagement in cities. With their expanding populations and active communities, cities have become hotbeds for innovation, especially when it comes to resolving urban challenges. Consider the example of the New York City Big Apps competition that has enabled that city to solicit software solutions for local issues from citizen developers who participate in the competition for a prize. The competition has been successfully executed by New York since 2009 and has gained much attention from local software developers interested in using the data made accessible by local city agencies to create solutions to problems. In 2013, more than 60 city agencies participated in the competition, which made more than 350 data sets available to the participants (La Vorgna et al., 2014). Through the competition, the city has been able to generate close to 250 software applications geared towards resolving various local issues ranging from parking, health and safety, public parks, and ease of accessibility of public transportation information. The example highlights how public agencies can leverage a critical resource—that is, the knowledge and skills of their citizens—to devise innovative solutions to local issues. In addition, the example also underlines the fact that citizens are co-creators and demonstrate interest in being positioned to contribute to their community.

With the number of cities worldwide expected to grow rapidly in terms of their geographic area and population, we expect greater interest in development and deployment of technology-enabled participatory platforms in cities (Desouza and Bhagwatwar, 2012; Dobbs et al., 2012). Deployment of technology-enabled platforms that promote citizen engagement, collaborative governance, and leveraging collective intelligence is a crucial underpinning of designing smarter cities (Desouza, 2014). Citizens and public agencies need to work collaboratively to build livable and sustainable environments. Towards this end, it becomes critical that we have platforms that promote innovation and collaboration. Currently, however, there is limited research on the form of these platforms and the dynamics involved in solving vexing local challenges. This paper seeks to fill this gap in the literature.

Technology-enabled participatory platforms represent the new wave of mechanisms that enable citizens to engage in local issues in more ways than before. This changing nature of civic engagement positions public administration and urban planning researchers to focus on these newly emerging technology-enabled participatory platforms. The limited theoretical understanding of technology-enabled participatory platforms calls for a need to develop frameworks and classifications that would help analyze these emerging platforms better. In this paper, we try to make a modest contribution towards exploring the form and function of technology-enabled participatory platforms in urban settings.

Employing a grounded theoretic approach (Strauss and Corbin, 1997) that relied on extensive secondary data analysis, we examined participatory platforms deployed in 21 of the 25 most populated cities within the United States. We studied the characteristics of these platforms, their components, the online behavior of citizens who participate on the platforms, the kinds of problems/decisions that are examined on these platforms, and the role these platforms are playing not only in better engaging citizens but also in influencing the public policy process. We describe the process of how collective citizen intelligence is leveraged on these platforms towards outcomes that advance the planning and governance of cities pursuing the goals of livability, economic vitality, and resilience. Based on our analysis, we posit four models that capture the variances in the communication and collaboration processes involved in the development, implementation, and use of these participatory platforms.

The four models advance our understanding of technology-enabled participatory platforms by explicating: (a) the nuances in the different phases, ranging from development to actual use, of different types of platforms; (b) the role of citizens and public agencies within each phase; and (c) differences in the goals of the platforms and any possible relationships of the platform goals with the known issues associated with a city.

The rest of the paper is organized as follows. In the next section, we briefly sketch the construct of civic engagement and discuss how technologies are changing the nature of civic engagement. Next, we define technology-enabled participatory platforms and walk through their components. Following that, we outline the four archetypes of technology-enabled participatory platforms we deduced from our research. We conclude the paper with a discussion of the implications and areas for future research.

Civic Engagement and Technologies

There is a growing consensus among researchers and practitioners alike that active civic engagement is critical for the design of participatory and inclusive governance mechanisms (Dahl, 1994; King et al., 1998; Irvin and Stansbury, 2004; Gaventa and Barrett, 2010). Civic engagement is defined as the individual and collective actions that are geared towards addressing issues of public concern (Shiller, 2013). Effective civic engagement requires public agencies to loosen the traditional reins of power and believe in the capabilities of citizens to actively participate and design governance mechanisms, institutions, and solutions (Shiller, 2013). Recent research has suggested that one of the major motivating factors for citizens to actively seek avenues for engagement is the cognitive surplus (Shirky, 2010). Cognitive surplus represents the amount of time citizens spend in contributing to activities that they see as potentially beneficial to themselves or to the community they live in (Shirky, 2010; Shirky and Pink, 2010). Given the sophisticated technology-mediated mechanisms of engagement available at their disposal, citizens are now able to easily contribute to causes that are of importance to them (Shirky and Pink, 2010). This form of engagement has become especially important for urban areas where rapid population growth has begun to strain existing infrastructures and vital resources. In such situations, the role of citizens who can use the available technological tools and resources to discuss and co-create innovative solutions to resolve local problems has become important (Desouza, 2014). While the nature of the co-created solutions developed by these citizens using their frugal resources might not be sophisticated, the solutions are still good enough to resolve the local issues without waiting for help from the local public agencies (Desouza, 2014).

Given the changing nature of civic engagement in recent years from the traditional forms such as town hall meetings to more active engagement through the recently emerging technology-enabled participatory platforms, it is important to consider the well-known conceptualizations of civic engagement from prior literature such as the Arnstein (1969) ladder of public participation. Arnstein (1969) provided a nuanced conceptualization of the range of public participation from non-participation to tokenism to citizen power. Non-participation, as the name implies, signifies no involvement by the public in the policy and planning processes. Tokenism has three sub-levels—informing, consultation, and placation. *Informing* refers to agencies keeping citizens informed about social issues. *Consultation* occurs when agencies solicit citizen input for decisions regarding social issues. While there is a degree of communication in the informing and consultation sub-dimensions, there is no certainty that the opinions of citizens will actually be considered by the authorities while they are making decisions. *Placation* calls for including people at positions in the policy process, such that they have influence over decisions being made. The third level, citizen power, which indicates the highest level of public participation, has three sub-levels—partnership, delegated power, and citizen control. *Partnership* calls for a collaborative alliance between the public and the public agencies in decision-making. *Delegated power* refers to an increased level of public independence in solving problems through delegation of authority by a public agency. The final level of *citizen control* indicates complete public control over the decision-making process. Other models on the topic are similar and have an evolution from no citizen participation, to agencies keeping citizens abreast of activities and events, followed by agencies soliciting citizen input, leading to agencies collaborating with citizens on information analysis and decision-making, and finally, citizens solving their own problems.

Recent scholarship in public administration has discussed issues related to the decrease in citizen engagement in public policy matters (Dalton, 2008; Kleinman et al., 2011). There is an overall shift in the nature of citizen engagement from real-world platforms such as democratic forums that address a variety of topics to interest-based online forums that empower citizens to participate in issues that are of interest to them (Kleinman et al., 2011). In contrast to situations in the past where citizens had little power to directly voice their concerns about the functioning of government, technology has empowered citizens to either act on their own to resolve their concerns or voice their opinions through diverse channels (Schachter, 1995). Urban Mechanics, an initiative by the cities of Boston and Philadelphia, is an example of such a forum. Through Urban Mechanics, citizens can convey their ideas about improving the city or any aspects of the functioning of the local government to the Mayor's Office. Through the initiative, the two cities have initiated and implemented more than 30 projects in areas such as education, transportation, and utilities. Some of the outcomes of the projects include convenient mobile applications for accessing transportation-related information, Internet-based forums for citizens to discuss local issues, and collaboration with national agencies and private firms to implement green building standards in the city.

Technology-enabled participatory platforms are being designed by the very people who live in these urban spaces and solve local problems where they live and work (Howe, 2006). Social and participatory urban platforms redefine how public agencies connect with citizens, foster thoughtful deliberation, and even streamline internal processes and service delivery (Howe, 2006). Many emerging urban technologies are built with the premise of crowdsourcing data, information, and solutions from a diverse set of users to advance one or more goals (Starbird, 2011; Desouza, 2012b).

Technology-Enabled Participatory Platforms

Systems theory (Bertalanffy, 1968; Churchman, 1971) suggests that in order to understand the functioning of any system, the nature of the component elements and their interaction with each other and the surrounding environment is important to consider. Essentially, each of the individual components exhibits specific behavior and has certain characteristics that influence other components of the system and influence the functioning of the system as a whole. Technology-enabled participatory platforms represent virtual canvases created to source, analyze, visualize, and share information, expertise, and solutions to advance issues and/or solve problems. As the name implies, participatory platforms involve *participation* among a collection of users. In the context of an urban setting, these users are individuals who interact with a city (e.g., residents, employees who work in the city, and visitors, among others). Building on the systems theory, in order to understand the functioning of these platforms, it is first essential to understand the specific components and their characteristics. The major components of technology-enabled platforms are: agents, attractors, mediums, flows, technological capabilities, and goals. Figure 1 shows the interaction among these components and considers the platform as the system entity where the interactions occur. The following paragraphs describe each component and the interaction between the various components of the platform.

To understand each of the components of a technology-enabled participatory platform, consider the example of Textizen that was discussed earlier. The first component represents *agents*, which represent the entities that participate on the platforms. Agents may be individuals (e.g., citizens, activists, etc.) or organizations (e.g., public agencies, non-governmental organizations, businesses, etc.). For example, on Textizen, agents represent citizens and the public agencies that use the platform for discussing various local issues. Agents interact with each other on the platform by exchanging resources and information (goods and services) with one another. Platforms differ in their level of exclusivity when it comes to which agents can participate on particular platforms. Some platforms are open and allow anyone to join. Others might be restricted, having current members recommend new members or have other pre-screening criteria before

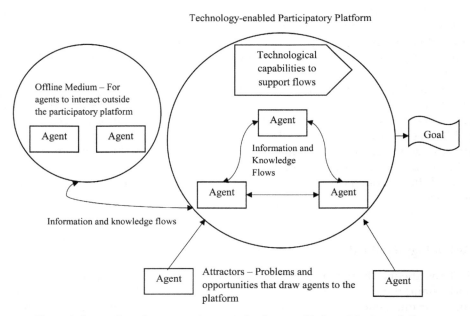

Figure 1: Interaction of components on a technology-enabled participatory platform.

one is allowed to participate. Textizen represents a platform that is open and allows anyone (citizens or public agency representatives) to join the platform.

Attractors are artifacts that mobilize the agents to participate on the platform. Attractors can be many things: (a) problems and opportunities that draw agents to the platform for stimulating conversation, ideating solutions, evaluating policy options, and collectively mobilizing offline; (b) *data made available* on the platform that agents have an interest in mining, analyzing, and participating in; (c) *data collected* through the platform that shows the citizen responses to specific issues to the users of the platform; or (d) the network of agents that participate on the platform. A network consisting of key individuals can draw others to the platform due to the potential for advancing a given cause or even just increasing one's own professional (and social) network. In the case of Textizen, attractors are the local problems and the opportunities to resolve those problem through the platform that motivate the citizens and public agency representatives to use the platform.

A key goal of participatory platforms is to facilitate information and knowledge *flows*. Without the promotion of effective and efficient information and knowledge transfer, the participatory platform will be limited in its ability to support civic engagement. For simplicity, *information* is the sharing of factual material, updates on projects and events, and data for planning and analysis. *Knowledge* represents opinions, expertise, and know-how that are shared on events, artifacts, and systems being considered by the community on the platform. Knowledge can be embedded into solutions that are exchanged on the platform. For example, citizens can share solutions that are the products of the application of their knowledge and expertise. Information and knowledge flows can take place between a given category of agents (e.g., citizens) or across multiple categories of agents (e.g., between citizens and public agencies). Information and knowledge flows can be centered on deliberations (i.e., discussion of issues) and participation (i.e., making decisions through tools such as voting, rating, etc.). In the case of Textizen, the information and knowledge flows occur between citizens and public agency representatives who use the platforms. As discussed earlier, the information and knowledge flows on Textizen can be centered around specific local issues (as well as being focused on decision-making processes such as voting/polls).

Technological capabilities found on a platform support flows and the achievement of goals. Capabilities found on the platform allow citizens to get to know one another, organize themselves into groups, share and debate ideas and solutions, vote on solutions, and share feedback on the overall operation of the platform. On Textizen, some of the technological capabilities include sending and receiving messages, creating surveys, and a dashboard that presents an analysis of the collected data. More advanced platforms include features like GPS tracking for situating information shared, based on locality, gaming features that allow citizens to compete with one another to advance a cause or solve a problem, and networking tools that plug into dominant social platforms such as Facebook, Twitter, LinkedIn, etc.

There are two main *mediums* on which a platform can be deployed—offline or online. Offline participatory platforms have been around since ancient times (e.g., the agora). This paper specifically focuses on platforms that operate online, i.e., are technology-enabled. Textizen is an example of such an online platform.

Platforms might choose to advance any number of objectives, but in most cases there is an overall goal that drives the creation of the platform. Some platforms are canvases to attract solutions to complex technological or social problems, while others might have a goal to raise awareness about particular social issues or causes. In the urban context, the goals of the platforms focus on improving one or more aspects of a city's physical infrastructure, governance mechanisms, or an issue affecting the city's future sustainability, livability, and vitality.

Methodology

We analyzed technology-enabled participatory platforms deployed in the 25 most populated US cities (US Census Bureau, 2012). We examined each platform's online presence and also reviewed secondary information, e.g., articles, press, and other media mentions. Our analysis focused on classifying the platforms based on the dominant *agents* on the platforms and the data/information flows among the agents. We focused on these two factors because they define aspects related to the collaborative environment of the platforms such as who controls behavior of other participants on the platform, how outputs generated on the platform are used by public agencies and/or citizens, and the type of outcomes from the platform (e.g., collective decisions, apps, offline campaigns, etc.).

Our search yielded 38 technology-enabled participatory platforms (See Table 1). Four out of the 25 cities—Los Angeles, Nashville, Phoenix, and El Paso—did not have any technology-enabled participatory platforms. We collected and tabulated a wide assortment of data elements on each platform such as the year of deployment, number of registered users, number of posts created by the users, primary goal of the platform, the supporting entity for the platform (public agencies, individual citizens, or citizen groups), and any examples of the solutions produced through the platforms. Upon closer examination we discarded 13 platforms due to the fact that they were not "participatory" but rather simply information conveyance platforms. An example of a platform we discarded from the final analysis is Crime in Chicago (www.crimeinchicago.org) that helps citizens visualize crimes that have occurred in the city. This platform does not provide any mechanisms for citizens to provide input or discuss any issues related to crimes in Chicago. Our final analysis included a total of 25 platforms from 16 of the 25 most populated cities (See Table 2).

In the tradition of grounded theory (Strauss and Corbin, 1997), we worked iteratively through the data collected on the platforms. Through open coding, we arrived at various variants of how collective intelligence was leveraged on technology-enabled platforms. Thereafter, we created archetypes of collective intelligence models. Next, two researchers studied each platform and classified into one of the four categories of technology-enabled platforms. We shared our findings with urban planners and public managers at three forums to seek input and refine our conceptualizations.

Four Archetypes of Technology-Enabled Participatory Platforms

We now describe four archetypes of technology-enabled participatory platforms. For each archetype, we share illustrative examples, and then describe the process of collaboration between the agents on the platform and the outcomes.

Table 1: List of technology-enabled participatory platforms.

City	Platform Name	Founders	Year	Goal
Austin	SpeakUpAustin	City of Austin	2010	Public agencies and citizens can post ideas/projects, discuss them, vote for ideas, and many ideas get implemented
Austin	ParkMe Austin	ParkMe	2012	Allows citizen to view real-time parking availability information and provide personal updates about parking
Austin	CivicIdeas	City of Austin	2011	Public agencies post issues on the platform, citizens then discuss the issues to come up with innovative solutions for implementation
Baltimore	StepUp!	Cities of Service	2010	Citizens discuss the top city issues (drug addiction, crime, and urban blight) and discuss possible solutions
Baltimore	Open311	City of Baltimore	2011	Provides easy access to 311 services enabling citizens to easily report local issues
Boston	Citizen's Connect	City of Boston	2010	Empowers citizens to be reporters on local issues. Government agencies can later take action on the reported issues
Boston	New Urban Mechanism	City of Boston	2010	Public agencies propose a wide array of projects where citizen-generated innovative ideas can be considered for project improvement
Boston	Boston Open Government	City of Boston	2010	Website enabling open access to city-related information
Boston	Localocracy	Conor White-Sullivan and Aaron Soules	2008	Enables people from a locality to discuss local problems, generate ideas to solve those problems, and select ideas based on the opinions of others
Charlotte	My Charlotte	City of Charlotte	2012	Application for easy access to city services.
Chicago	Crime in Chicago	Open City	2012	Website to make available crime information easily to Chicago residents
Columbus	Ohio Citizen Action	Citizen group in Columbus	1975	Aims at engaging citizens in various pollution-reducing and preventing initiatives. The website has apps available for phones as well as a presence on social networks. However, most of the action takes place offline

Table 1: Continued

City	Platform Name	Founders	Year	Goal
Dallas	Green Dallas	Not available	2011	Enables citizens to get information and collaborate on different kinds of green initiatives including air quality and green energy. Most of the projects are initiated by independent organizations rather than individual citizens.
Denver	Citizens for a Safer Denver	Citizen group in Denver	2008	Citizens discuss the issue of safer marijuana laws with the goal of coming up with effective solutions
Denver	A+ Denver—Citizens for Denver Schools	Formed through an initiative by the Mayor of City of Denver	2006	Aims to make Denver's citizens aware of the efforts of school reform. A+ Denver members are composed of community and business leaders, parents, representatives from local foundations, and universities.
Fort Worth	Fort Worth Ideas	Cathy Hirt	2009	Local issues identified by public and government are discussed with the goal of coming up with innovative solutions
Houston	MyCity Houston	My City Houston	2010	Platform for the city to make useful information easily accessible to citizens in one place. The information is provided about services by range of department including the police, 311 or utility services, housing information.
Indianapolis	Indy Downtown App	Indianapolis Downtown Inc.	2011	Citizens discuss various city issues such as parking and utilities and other elements like shopping malls. There is no solution generation here since issues are just shared not ideated upon.
Jacksonville	JaxReady	City of Jacksonville	2011	Provides information to citizens regarding natural disasters, extreme weather conditions, and other emergency issues.
Kansas	Kansas Transportation Online Community	Kansas Department of Transportation	2009	Facilitates conversations on transportation-related issues among citizens in Kansas.

(Continued)

Table 1: Continued

City	Platform Name	Founders	Year	Goal
Memphis	Smart Gov	City of Memphis	2012	Citizens report problems to public agencies as they notice them. Public agencies take action on the reported issues later.
New York, Chicago	SeeClickFix	Local city government	2010	Forum for people to report local issues that are directed to concerned public agencies for immediate action.
New York	Change by Us NYC	City of New York	2011	Generation of solutions for common problems through citizen collaboration
New York	New York Big Apps	City of New York and CollabFinder	2009	Platform where citizens can access open data and develop applications that effectively use open data. Public agencies provide monetary incentive for application development
New York	New York Health Ratings	Aaron Dancygier	2011	Generation of solutions for common problems through citizen collaboration
New York	Mintscraps	Tony Vu	2012	Helps restaurants, grocery stores, and other food service establishments reduce their waste disposal fees. The website helps restaurant owners connect with city waste haulers and consultants to find opportunities for savings in their waste streams.
New York	NYC Open Data	City of New York	2011	NYC Open Data contains data sets produced by various NYC agencies and other city organizations. This platform is intended more for informational purposes for citizens rather than collaboration.
San Francisco	Crimespotting	Mike Migurski	2007	Provides an interface that helps easily access data about crime incidents
Philadelphia	PhillyRising Collaborative	City of Philadelphia	2011	Targets neighborhoods in the city that are plagued by chronic crime and quality of life concerns, and establishes partnerships with community members to address these issues.
Philadelphia	Technically Philly	City of Philadelphia	2012	Enables citizens to report local issues using phone features such as cameras and GPS.

(Continued)

Table 1: Continued

City	Platform Name	Founders	Year	Goal
Philadelphia	Philly KEYSPOT	City of Philadelphia	2011	Provides Easy and free Internet access, computer training to Philadelphia locals. About 41 percent of Philadelphia citizens do not have access to the Internet. The initiative aims at resolving this issue.
San Antonio	Cellular on Patrol	City of San Antonio (Police Department)	2011	Allows citizens to report information about crime incidents
San Antonio	Tip 411	City of San Antonio (Police Department)	2011	Provides web-based form for citizens to provide information about any tips they have for police, or information about incidents in the city.
San Antonio	San Antonio City Connect	City of San Antonio	2011	Enables citizens to report issues about various matters and discuss those issues. The forum makes the top and recent issues visible easily by pushing them to the top. The forum also has discrete categorization of issues based on issue types.
San Jose	@SanJoseCitizen	City of San Jose	2010	Used to convey useful information to citizens and also gets any feeds from them.
San Jose	San Jose Citizen Space	Citizen Space	2012	Enables citizens having flexible work schedules to share their working spaces. Citizens also organize professional events and activities geared towards developing innovative solutions to local issues.
Seattle	Envision Seattle	Citizens group in Seattle	2011	Initiative by citizens to eliminate corporate funding in elections. Aims at just creating awareness about the issue, and so is only for informational purposes
Washington DC	Apps for Development	iStrategyLabs	2008	Provides a platform for public agencies to post problems and citizens to develop solution for those problems. Public agencies provide monetary incentives for application development

Model 1: Citizen-Centric and Citizen-Sourced Data

Localocracy (www.localocracy.com) harnesses citizen intelligence for creating solutions for social problems by enabling people from a particular locality to discuss local issues, generate ideas to solve those issues, and select ideas based on the opinion of others (Desouza and Bhagwatwar, 2012). Once citizens are confident about the effectiveness and feasibility of their solutions, they can propose the solutions to the appropriate public agency. Localocracy invites public agency representatives to actively monitor citizen suggestions on local issues, thereby providing an opportunity for citizens to propose their solutions to problems directly to the public agency. The acceptance and implementation of the solution remains at the discretion of the public agency. Localocracy, initially available only in Amherst, was later made accessible across multiple cities in Massachusetts including Arlington, Cambridge, Granby, Milford, and South Hadley.

Change by Us Philly (www.philly.changeby.us) is an online marketplace for community projects that provides participants with an opportunity to share ideas for making their city better. The project was launched by CEOs for Cities, Local Projects, and Code for America in collaboration with the City of Philadelphia. The platform provides citizens with an avenue to suggest the changes they would like to see in their city and then take action through grassroots projects and community collaboration. Participants are provided with a chance to suggest "ideas" or join "projects" depending on their interest. Ideas are reviewed by a network of city leaders that guides projects. The Change by Us Philly platform has a simple interface that enables participants to join discussion forums of their interest as well as create new forums whenever necessary. Participants can leverage the platform's project management tools to recruit volunteers, promote events, and find in-kind donations. Participants can also form small groups to discuss issues of common concern as the site helps you find people by interest, location, and skills. In addition, the platform also contains information on public and non-profit programs that can help tap into the power of community, local knowledge, and connect with city services. A total of 512 ideas, 100 projects, and 67 resources had been submitted by the public on the platform (as of July 21, 2013).

The process of leveraging collective citizen intelligence under the *citizen-centric and citizen-sourced data* model is as follows. The first step is the realization of the need to solve a local issue by citizens. Citizens represent the actors that are motivated to solve one or more local issues. The local issues, and in fact, the physical geography of the issues, serve as the attractor. These platforms have emerged as an alternative medium for citizens to organize themselves to make a difference in their local communities. The local issue in this case acts as an attractor. The second step is to harness citizen intelligence to design innovative solutions for the local issue. The third step involves refining and evaluating solutions by the citizens using the technological features provided by the platform such as discussion boards and opinion polls. Finally, vetted solutions are moved to public agencies for their consideration and implementation. The choice and implementation of the solution is at the discretion of the public agencies.

Citizens, the principal actors on these platforms, are motivated by the goal of contributing their idea towards solving local governance challenges. Private actors not only develop the platform, but also are the primary providers of information, expertise, and solutions that are shared on the platform. Local govern-

Table 2: Analysis of the platforms based on the components framework.

City	Name of Platform	Attractors	Medium	Primary Information and Knowledge flows	Technological features	Overall Framework
Austin	ParkMe Austin	Information access and sharing	Online Only	Citizen-Citizen	Real-time information feeds	Model 1
Baltimore	StepUp!	Local issues	Online and Offline	Citizen-Citizen	Discussion board	Model 1
Boston	Citizen's Connect	Local issues	Online Only	Citizen-Citizen	Discussion board, voting tools	Model 1
Boston	Localocracy	Local issues	Online Only	Citizen-Citizen	Discussion board, voting tool	Model 1
Columbus	Ohio Citizen Action	Local issues	Online and Offline	Citizen-Citizen	Website and social network integration	Model 1
Dallas	Green Dallas	Local issues	Online and Offline	Citizen-Citizen	Website only	Model 1
Denver	Citizens for a Safer Denver	Local issues	Online and Offline	Citizen-Citizen	Website for information conveyance	Model 1
Indianapolis	Indy Downtown App	Information access and sharing	Online Only	Citizen-Citizen	Discussion board	Model 1
Memphis	Smart Gov	Local issues	Online Only	Citizen-Citizen	Discussion forum and e-mails/messaging	Model 1
New York, Chicago	SeeClickFix	Local issues	Online Only	Government-Citizen	Discussion board, voting tool	Model 1
New York	Change by Us NYC	Local issues	Online Only	Citizen-Citizen	Discussion board, voting tool	Model 1
New York	Mintscraps	Information access and sharing	Online Only	Citizen-Citizen	Discussion board, interactive analysis tools	Model 1
Philadelphia	PhillyRising Collaborative	Local issues	Online and Offline	Citizen-Citizen	Website and discussion board	Model 1
San Antonio	Tip 411	Local issues	Online Only	Government-Citizen	Website and online forms	Model 1
San Antonio	San Antonio City Connect	Local issues	Online Only	Citizen-Citizen	Discussion board, voting tool, post sorting	Model 1
San Jose	San Jose Citizen Space	Information access and sharing	Online and Offline	Citizen-Citizen	Website and discussion board	Model 1

New York	New York Health Ratings	Information access and sharing	Online Only	Government-Citizen	Maps, discussion board	Model 2
San Francisco	Crimespotting	Local issues	Online Only	Government-Citizen	Maps, comments	Model 2
Austin	CivicIdeas	Local issues	Online Only	Government-Citizen	Discussion board, voting tool	Model 3
Austin	SpeakUpAustin	Local issues	Online only	Government-Citizen	Discussion board, voting tool	Model 3
Boston	New Urban Mechanism	Local issues	Online Only	Government-Citizen	Discussion board, voting tools	Model 3
Fort Worth	Fort Worth Ideas	Local issues	Online Only	Government-Citizen	Discussion board, voting tool	Model 3
Kansas	Kansas Transportation Online Community	Local issues	Online Only	Government-Citizen	Website, daily news feed, and discussion board	Model 3
New York	New York Big Apps	Local issues, monetary incentives	Online only	Government-Citizen	Voting tool, discussion board, calendar	Model 4
Washington DC	Apps for Development	Local issues, monetary incentives	Online Only	Government-Citizen	Discussion board, voting tool, submission system	Model 4

ment agencies play a passive role. They receive information and solutions once they are vetted by the local community and are not bound to implement the solutions offered. In some cases, such as Change by Us Philly, public agencies are spectators at best.

Model 2: Citizen-Centric and Government Open Data

In 2007, Mike Migurski, the technology director at Stamen Design, realized the need to increase awareness about criminal activity in Oakland, California, and developed the Oakland Crimespotting application (Forrest, 2009). This application provides the most up-to-date information about criminal incidents that take place within Oakland. Citizens can also leave comments about an incident. The ability to instantly access data about crime incidents allows citizens to take required precautionary steps to keep themselves safe. The application uses open data from law enforcement agencies and displays that information on an interactive map. Citizens are able to track the crime by different localities and have the provision of tracking crimes based on type. Even after the initial success of the application, the city government decided to cut off the data stream for the application, saying that the frequent data demands of the application were disrupting the city's crime website (Miller, 2009). However, owing to the popularity of the application, the city government not only reversed its decision but also decided to support the application by providing monetary and infrastructural support. The city used the platform to receive additional information from citizens about criminal activity and to help law enforcement agencies track criminal activity. The immense success of the application for Oakland motivated Stamen Design to design a similar application for the San Francisco region (Oakland Crimespotting, 2009). The website, which was launched in August 2009, was well received by the citizens of San Francisco and also received support from Mayor Newsom and local law enforcement agencies (Miller, 2009).

In March 2011, Aaron Dancygier launched the NYC Health Ratings website (www.nychealthratings.com) with the goal of giving easy access to citizens about the health safety ratings of any restaurant in the city. The platform relies on datasets from the New York City Department of Health and Mental Hygiene which conducts inspections of city restaurants and gives them a health safety rating. The data set includes data for about 25,000 restaurants in the city. The platform has an easy-to-navigate map interface along with a search box that allows a user to research the restaurant of her choice and know about its health safety ratings. A forum exists to facilitate discussion on various restaurants and neighborhoods in New York City that are rated high or low on health safety ratings. A top 10 best and worst neighborhoods in the city based on the health safety ratings is available. The platform can be accessed on mobile phones and integrates with existing websites such as Yelp and Foursquare. The platform received special recognition in the New York Big Apps competition in 2011 in the eating and health category.

The examples of Oakland Crimespotting and NYC Health Ratings point to the second model—*citizen centric and government open data* model. Like the preceding model, citizens represent the focal actors. The key attractor is open data that is analyzed, visualized, and made easily accessible to users. Information flows are mostly characterized by citizens interacting with the platform and with the data on it. Limited citizen-to-citizen or even citizen-agency interaction is present. Citizens use the platform to seek information they need and may at times provide data (e.g., in the form of feedback, comments, suggestions) that are then available to other users of the systems. Citizens share knowledge and expertise as they design the platform. The goal of most of these platforms is to raise awareness of social issues through increasing transparency and information access.

Once a participatory platform is designed and implemented, public agencies react and provide feedback. In case of Crimespotting, the city government initially criticized the platform before eventually adopting it as a solution. In the case of New York Health Ratings, the New York Big Apps competition recognized it as a critical innovation. The difference between this model and the *citizen-centric and citizen-sourced data* model is the way solution implementation is executed. Crimespotting and New York Health Ratings had already been deployed without seeking permission from a public agency. Citizens do not rely on public agencies to deploy solutions they come up with. They implement them, and then agencies can react to them.

Model 3: Government-Centric and Citizen-Sourced Data

SpeakUpAustin (www.austintexas.icanmakeitbetter.com), developed and implemented by the City of Austin, is an application that engages citizens on social issues. Local problems identified by public agencies are posted on the application. Problems are organized into categories (e.g., public transportation, utilities, waste). Citizens can read any of the posted problems and propose ideas to resolve them. The public can also vote for the posted solutions. By generating awareness about local problems, public agencies aim to foster citizen engagement for effective decision-making. The platform solicits citizen participation primarily during the idea generation and voting stages. The decision whether to implement the solution or not, the timeframe, and budget decisions about implementation are made by the public agency. Even during the implementation phase, the public agency can solicit citizen feedback and use the application to keep citizens updated about the progress. SpeakUpAustin was launched in the summer of 2011 and has already accumulated more than 1,300 registered users, more than 450 new ideas, around 1,000 comments, and more than 4,500 votes on various issues.

Kansas Transportation Online Community (K-TOC) is an online forum launched by the Kansas Department of Transportation in 2009. The goal for the development of K-TOC was to facilitate conversations on transportation-related issues among citizens in Kansas (Kansas Department of Transportation, 2009). The platform not only helps agencies convey important information to citizens but also lets them raise any concerns and discuss them. Some of the public agency officials who actively monitor and participate on the forum include road supervisors, flight operators, city and county engineers, airport managers, and public work directors. Through the platform, daily news stories, updates on transportation projects and informative blogs by transportation experts are made available to citizens. The discussion forum is a place for citizens and public agency officials to collaborate. Public agency officials post information about upcoming transportation projects on the forum on which they would like to solicit public opinion. Citizen-proposed solutions are considered by public agency officials for refinement and implementation. T-Link, the task force organized by the Governor, which was charged with developing new approaches to transportation, uses the platform to further citizen engagement on upcoming transportation infrastructure projects.

The *government-centric and citizen information model* is an example of how public agencies can take the lead to leverage collective citizen intelligence through design and implementation of participatory platforms. Through the creative use of technology, local agencies can solicit citizen feedback and engage in ideation for solutions. Similar to the *citizen-centric and citizen-sourced data* model, implementation of the solution is at the discretion of the public agency. The *government-centric and citizen information model* involves public agencies and citizens as near-equal actors. The attractor for both these actors is the common goal of resolving a local problem. As such, the flow of information is bi-directional.

During the initial phase, the flow of information is from the public agencies to the citizens. In the examples discussed above, the City of Austin and the Kansas Department of Transportation communicated the availability of the platform to citizens. The public agencies have to market the platform to citizens as a viable space for dialogue, deliberation, and collaborative decision-making. The platform's features such as news feeds, blogs, and discussion boards help in this conveyance of information. After the information is conveyed from public agencies, the flow of information and knowledge is between citizens. Citizens use the discussion board and other media features to share their ideas, opinions, and judgments on solutions. The convergence features provided by the forum such as the voting and polling tools help citizens rank and evaluate solutions. These solutions are then passed on to the public agencies. The final stage of the process involves decision making on the part of the public agency on whether to implement the community suggestions or not.

Model 4: Government-Centric and Citizen-Developed Solutions

In September 2008, Vivek Kundra, the former Chief Technology Officer for Washington, DC asked iStrategyLabs to suggest a way to design an open data catalog useful for citizens, developers, and public agencies (Corbett, 2008). Instead of investing many years and millions of dollars in contracts with private organizations to develop technological solutions to address local issues based on open data, iStrategyLabs employed an approach that leveraged citizen intelligence. The competition made available a vast amount of city data to citizens. The response from citizens was overwhelming. Within 30 days of the competition's launch iStrategyLabs received 47 web-based or smart phone-based applications—an estimated net value of close to $2.3 million (Corbett, 2008). Communities of developers and citizens came forward to create innovative solutions to solve the city's problems. After the applications were submitted, a joint panel of citizens and government officials was asked to select applications for the different prize categories. Based on the panel's decisions and votes of citizens, prizes were given to the best applications in various categories such as social applications and community grants.

Initiated in 2011, New York Big Apps is an annual competition that solicits innovative solutions in the form of smart phone and web-based applications from developers based on the open data made available by New York City.

Many of these datasets were previously under-analyzed or unanalyzed due to a lack of resources, limited budgets, and public agencies focusing on other priorities. The competition exploits crowdsourcing by asking enthusiastic developers to come forward and develop applications. The developers have access to more than 170 data sets made available by over 30 city public agencies. Developers are also allowed to communicate and collaborate with each other during the application development process. To incentivize the developers, cash prizes are also made available to winners and runner-ups; NYC Big Apps 2013 offers $150,000 in cash prizes across various application categories. The various areas in which applications can be developed include education, health, clean energy, resilience and environment, public transportation, and utilities, among others. Citizens vote for their favorite apps, and a panel of judges select the winning submission in each category.

The above examples show how public agencies and citizens can work together to create innovative solutions through participatory platforms. This represents the *government-centric and citizen app* model. The model requires mutual participation from both public agencies and citizens. The first step is the realization of the need to solve local problems and for the public agency to solicit citizen help. The second step is leveraging collective citizen intelligence to design innovative solutions for the problem. In the case of the Apps for Development example, once the competition was announced by iStrategyLabs, communities of developers and citizens created applications that addressed various local issues. In the case of the New York Big Apps competition, once the competition was launched by New York City, individual groups worked on their applications using the data sets made available by public agencies to create novel applications. In both examples, as the applications were developed, they were submitted to the competitions for judging and voting. Again, the top solutions from the submitted solution pool were selected based on the opinion of judges and citizens. This was achieved through a voting process. Once the top solutions were selected, the solutions were given prizes and public recognition. In addition, the implementation of the applications occurred through cooperation between citizens and public agencies. A key difference between this model and the *government-centric and citizen information* model is that the outputs are actual solutions (e.g., mobile applications) developed by the citizens rather than ideas or information, which is the output of model 3. The primary actors in this model are the public agency and the citizens involved in the process of creating the mobile application. Similar to the previous models, the attractor in this case is, again, the motivation to resolve local problems using an innovative approach. Citizen developers are attracted by the opportunity to demonstrate their skills in developing applications that can help resolve local problems. The monetary incentive provided by the public agency is another attractor motivating citizen developers to engage in the application development process.

Analysis of Models

Table 2 outlines the technology-enabled participatory platforms that we analyzed to arrive at our four archetypes. The four models vary in their focus and their approaches to leveraging citizen intelligence for tackling urban problems and realizing opportunities. As outlined above, both parties, citizens and public agencies, can take the initiative to create the platform. Public agencies can play a key role in incentivizing the process in the form of monetary prizes and by making data available to citizens. The platforms of Models 1 and 3 are popular among cities (See Table 2). It is interesting to note that in cities where local governments have not created participatory platforms, citizens have stepped up and designed their own platforms.

Model 1—*citizen-centric and citizen-sourced data*—and Model 2—*citizen centric and government open data*—capture a collaboration process that is dominated by citizen-to-citizen information flows. A noticeable aspect of these models is that the role of public agencies is passive during most of the process. In both models, citizens interact with each other to discuss the problems and share information about it. The platform facilitates access to the sharing of information. Since the citizens play a dominant role in most aspects of the model, the platforms need to incorporate information conveyance, convergence, as well as networking features. Often, the platforms incorporate multiple features to provide multiple methods of communication and collaboration to the citizens. For example, the various conveyance features that the platforms in these models incorporate could include discussion boards, news feeds, posts, and rich media such as images. These conveyance features facilitate information exchange. The convergence features such as opinion polls and online voting systems help citizens make decision about a particular issue. In addition, the networking features such as personal profiles and discussions through comments and posts help citizens get to know each other better.

A critical difference between the two models is the source of data. While Model 1 data are generated by the citizens during the collaboration process, the data in Model 2 are provided by the public agency. Consequently, platforms represented by Model 2 are launched in a ready-to-use fashion, i.e., data have been analyzed, visualized, and made available in a form that facilitates its use. On the other hand, the platforms represented by Model 1 have minimal or no data at the outset of the project. Once citizens start interacting and actively participating on the platform, the data are generated. One reason many Model 1 platforms fail is their inability to generate data through citizen input and collaboration during the early days after launch. Designers of these platforms should ensure that they not only invest time in building the technology but also spend an equal amount of energy creating a community of users who are willing to use the platform. One strategy that we have found to be quite successful is for the platform to be launched in several stages, i.e., pre-alpha, alpha, beta soft launch, and then go live. During each of these stages content can be created, a network of users can be engaged, and bugs can be worked out.

Model 3—*government-centric and citizen-sourced data*—and Model 4—*government-centric and citizen-developed solutions*—deviate from Model 1 and Model 2 in many aspects. While Model 1 and Model 2 are dominated by information and knowledge exchange among citizens, Models 3 and 4 involve substantial government-citizen interactions. Model 3 platforms incorporate features that not only enable effective citizen-citizen interaction but also include conveyance capabilities that help citizens communicate with the relevant public agency quickly. Model 4 platforms source tangible solutions to urban problems and challenges. Most Model 4 platforms create technology-centric solutions such as mobile apps. In these settings, citizens and public agencies invest the greatest amount of time and energy to advance solutions.

The four archetypes represent different levels of citizen and public agency participation. Analyzing the archetypes using the well-known Arnstein ladder provides further insights into the role of the citizens in the process and how the four archetypes map onto the different participation levels as defined by Arnstein. Figure 2 shows the classification of the four archetypes within Arnstein's levels of participation.

Model 1 can be categorized under the tokenism-consultation level in the Arnstein model. The consultation level captures public agency-citizen interactions where public agencies solicit citizen inputs on various issues, but might or might not consider their inputs during any decision-making processes. Consequently, Model 1 implies a limited interaction between citizens and public agencies where although the solutions generated through the participatory platforms are communicated to the concerned public agencies, the implementation of the solution remains the discretion of the public agency. Similar to Model 1, Model 2 can also be categorized under the tokenism-consultation level. A key difference between the two models is the way in which consultation occurs. While in Model 1, the citizens have to take an initiative to communicate the solutions generated on the platform to the concerned public agencies, in Model 2, the public agencies take the initiative to make the data available to the citizens for use on the platform. Citizens analyze the data made available in order to come up with collective solutions for a problem. However, in both models, the decision to implement the generated solution is taken by the public agency. Citizens do not have any role to play in the decision-making process.

Model 3 can be categorized under the tokenism-placation level. Platforms in Model 3 require public agencies to take initiatives that would invite citizens to contribute any relevant information/data regarding a problem and possibly generate collective solutions for the problem. Going beyond just facilitating collaboration with citizens, public agencies often actively monitor the participatory platform and implement any solutions generated through the platform. Consequently, Model 3 implies a higher level of citizen participation in the decision-making processes than Models 1 and 2. Model 4 can be classified under the citizen power-partnership level. The participatory platforms in Model 4 require a significant amount of collaboration between citizens and public agencies. Public agencies have to take initiatives to facilitate citizen participation by creating incentives such as prizes, making data easily accessible, and creating avenues for

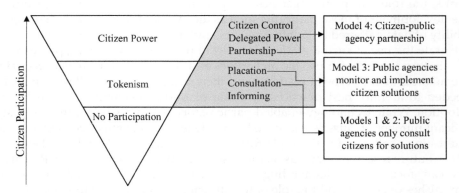

Figure 2: Classification of the four archetypes within the Arnstein framework.

direct interaction between citizens and public agencies. The public agencies expect to use the participatory platforms created by the citizens as a mainstream technology for soliciting citizen opinion in policy-making processes. In addition, the public agencies also define specific areas where they need the help of citizens. Consequently, the platforms in Model 4 require an ongoing effort by both the citizens and public agencies to find problems, develop solutions to resolve those problems, and implement the solutions.

Discussion

While there is no doubt that technology-enabled participatory platforms are here to stay, it is important to understand some of the limitations and unintended consequences of the use of these platforms. Citizen engagement through these platforms might slow down the pace of decision-making for public agencies and add complexities in the policy design and implementation processes (Lowndes et al., 2001; Carpini et al., 2004). Another issue that arises is that of social selectivity, i.e., when the distribution of engagement is uneven across the various social strata (Hilger, 2004; Carpini et al., 2004). Digital divide issues, including the inability to access the platforms and/or use the platforms effectively, can also curtail effective civic engagement (DiMaggio et al., 2004; Hargittai and Hinnant 2008). In addition, factors such as age, income, social status, skills, and even location might negatively influence civic engagement and eventually lead to situations where the interests or opinions of a few dominate those of the majority (Hargittai and Hinnant, 2008).

The four archetypes described in this paper highlight an underlying issue in the way the participatory platforms function and are developed and deployed. Most of the platforms are not produced through collaborative efforts between citizens and public agencies. In fact, many of the platforms were developed in adversarial conditions where an individual developer worked on the platform before it became popular. Given the potential benefits that these platforms offer for citizens and public agencies, it is important for public agencies to (a) create multiple avenues such as conferences and prize-based challenges that would give platform developers an opportunity to showcase their platforms, and (b) provide support. In addition, public administration researchers can focus on investigating the changes in policy structures necessary to support the development of such platforms, the role that public agencies can play to resolve the issues faced during the development of these platforms such as the availability of open data or accessibility of data gathered by public agencies, and how public agencies can possibly integrate the use of such a platform as part of public policy-making processes.

Future research can use the archetypes as a framework for further analyzing the nuances of each type of platform and their success measures. Research is also needed to identify best practices to guide platform development, launch, and adoption. While technology-enabled participatory platforms have attracted a significant number of citizens and have been able to generate effective outcomes, an interesting challenge for these platforms is sustainability (Mergel and Desouza, 2013). Future research can focus on the sustainability of these platforms. Researchers can focus on understanding how a platform's membership grows or diminishes over time and the role of the attractors that influence the membership levels. In addition, researchers can also conduct longitudinal studies to understand the relationship between the growth (or decline) in the number of participants on a platform, the number of local issues identified, and the number of solutions develop to resolve those issues. Essentially, while the membership of a platform might or might not grow over time, its effectiveness in identifying local problems and developing collective solutions for the problems would dictate if the platform would remain significant for concerned public agencies.

Finally, in addition to the discussed development and deployment issues related to the participatory platforms, it is also important for future research to develop measures or frameworks that can be used to assess the legitimacy of the participatory platforms. While numerous platforms might emerge, it is important to know the factors that can be used to understand the legitimacy of solutions developed on the platform. For example, it might be important for a public agency to consider solutions/recommendations from only those platforms that have a certain percentage of the local population actively engaged on the platform. As the number of participatory platforms for various cities continues to grow, it is important for public agencies to recognize the participatory platforms that are gaining prominence within the local community. Given their limited resources, public agencies can actively monitor and potentially form collaborations with only a limited number of platforms. Consequently, it becomes important for public agencies to understand which platforms are legitimate and sustainable. Future research can use the four archetypes proposed in this paper to investigate factors that public agencies can consider to assess which platforms would be most beneficial in terms of forming sustained collaboration with and leveraging most from the enthusiasm of the citizens participating in local issues.

Conclusion

We have only scratched the surface in examining technology-enabled participatory platforms. The four archetypes provide researchers with a framework for clear categorization of participatory platforms. By understanding the dominant actors for a platform and the pattern of information flows, researchers can categorize a platform into one of the four types. The four archetypes provide a guideline for future research to understand the temporal nature of stages that constitute the development and use of a platform. From the analyses presented in the paper, it is evident that the development, implementation, and eventual effective use of platforms follows a specific sequence of events that differ across the four archetypes. Public agencies and public managers need to appreciate the emergence of technology-enabled participatory platforms and their role in shaping, implementing, and evaluating policy and designing governance mechanisms. We expect the number of citizen-initiated technology-enabled platforms to rise significantly in the future, and the credibility and legitimacy of these platforms to increase as well.

Acknowledgments

Previous versions of this paper were presented at the 2012 IGU Commission on Geography of Governance Annual Conference, 2012 Americas Conference on Information Systems and the 2013 American Society for Public Administration Conference. We thank the audience for feedback received. Alison Sutherland, Titiana Ertiö, Kendra Smith, Rashmi Krishnamurthy, Jusil Lee, and Jaimy Alex provided valuable feedback and contributions to previous drafts of the paper. Kevin C. Desouza acknowledges partial funding for this work from the IBM Center for the Business of Government and the Alliance for Innovation. Any opinions, findings, and conclusions or recommendations expressed in this material are those of the authors and do not necessarily reflect the views of the IBM or the Alliance for Innovation. All errors and omissions are solely our responsibility.

Bibliography

S. Arnstein, "A Ladder of Citizen Participation," *Journal of the American Institute of Planners* 35 (1969) 216–224.

L.V. Bertalanffy, *General System Theory: Foundations, Development, Applications* (New York: Braziller, 1968) 141.

B. Bimber, "Measuring the Gender Gap on the Internet," *Social Science Quarterly* 81: 3 (2000) 868–876.

D.M.X. Carpini, F. Cook, and L.R. Jacobs, "Public Deliberation, Discursive Participation, and Citizen Engagement: A Review of the Empirical Literature," *Annual Review of Political Science* 7: 1 (2004) 315–344.

C.W. Churchman, *The Design of Inquiring Systems* (New York: Basic Books, 1971).

F. Corbett, Apps for Democracy Innovation Content. http://istrategylabs.com/work/apps-for-democracy-contest Accessed July 22, 2013, 2008.

R.A. Dahl, "A Democratic Dilemma: System Effectiveness versus Citizen Participation," *Political Science Quarterly* 109: 1 (1994) 23–34.

R.J. Dalton, "Citizenship Norms and the Expansion of Political Participation," *Political Studies* 56: 1 (2008) 76–98.

K.C. Desouza, Getting Serious About Resilience in Planning. http://www.planetizen.com/node/57827 Accessed July 22, 2013, 2012a.

K.C. Desouza, "Challenge.Gov: Using Competitions and Awards to Spur Innovation." http://www.businessofgovernment.org/sites/default/files/Challenge.gov_.pdf Accessed July 22, 2013, 2012b.

K.C. Desouza, "Our Fragile Emerging Megacities: A Focus on Resilience," http://www.planetizen.com/node/67338 Accessed July 7, 2014, 2014.

K.C. Desouza and A. Bhagwatwar, "Citizen Apps to Solve Complex Urban Problems," *Journal of Urban Technology* 19: 3 (2012): 107–136.

P. DiMaggio, E. Hargittai, C. Celeste, and S. Shafer, *Digital Inequality: From Unequal Access to Differentiated Use*. Social Inequality (New York: Russell Sage Foundation, 2004) 355–400.

S. Dirks and M. Keeling, "A Vision of Smarter Cities: How Cities can Lead the Way into a Prosperous and Sustainable Future," http://www-03.ibm.com/press/attachments/IBV_Smarter_Cities_-_Final.pdf Accessed July 8, 2014, 2009.

R. Dobbs, J. Remes, J. Manyika, C. Roxburgh, S. Smit, and F. Schaer, "Urban World: Cities and the Rise of the Consuming Class."http://www.mckinsey.com/insights/urbanization/urban_world_cities_and_the_rise_of_the_consuming_class Accessed July 8, 2014, 2012.

B. Forrest, "Seeing the Future of Mapping in Crimespotting," http://radar.oreilly.com/2009/08/seeing-the-future-mapping-crimespotting-stamen.html Accessed July 22, 2013, 2009.

J. Gaventa and G. Barrett, "So What Difference Does it Make? Mapping the Outcomes of Citizen Engagement," www.ids.ac.uk/files/dmfile/Wp347.pdf Accessed July 22, 2013, 2010.

E. Hargittai and A. Hinnant, "Digital Inequality Differences in Young Adults' Use of the Internet," *Communication Research* 35: 5 (2008) 602–621.

P. Hilger, "Civic Engagement of Marginalised Groups: Educational Aspects and Public Representation," www.mv.helsinki.fi/home/hilger/downloads/pdf/Hilger_GEA2004.pdf Accessed July 22, 2013, 2004.

J. Howe, "The Rise of Crowdsourcing," *Wired Magazine* 14: 6 (2006) 1–4.

A.I. Irvin and J. Stansbury, "Citizen Participation in Decision Making: Is It Worth the Effort?," *Public Administration Review* 64: 1 (2004) 55–65.

M.K. Jennings and V. Zeitner, "Internet Use and Civic Engagement: A Longitudinal Analysis," *Public Opinion Quarterly* 67: 3 (2003) 311–334.

Kansas Department of Transportation, "Kansas Launches Online Community to Discuss Transportation Issues," http://www.ksdot.org/PDF_Files/K-TOC%20launched.pdf Accessed July 22, 2013, 2009.

C.S. King, K.M. Fetley, and B.O. Susel, "The Question of Participation: Toward Authentic Public Participation in Public Administration," *Public Administration Review* 58 (1998) 317–326.

D.L. Kleinman, J.A. Delborne, and A.A. Anderson, "Engaging Citizens: The High Cost of Citizen Participation in High Technology," *Public Understanding of Science* 20: 2 (2011) 221–240.

M. La Vorgna, J. Wood, P. Muncie, and N. Sbordone, "Mayor Bloomberg Launches Fourth Annual Nyc Bigapps Competition," http://www1.nyc.gov/office-of-the-mayor/news/105–13/mayor-bloomberg-launches-fourth-annual-nyc-bigapps-competition Accessed July 1, 2014, 2013.

V. Lowndes, L. Pratchett, and G. Stoker, "Trends in Public Participation: Part 1–Local Government Perspectives," *Public Administration* 79: 1 (2001) 205–222.

I. Mergel and K.C. Desouza, "Implementing Open Innovation in the Public Sector: The Case of Challenge.Gov," *Public Administration Review* 73: 6 (2013) 882–890.

C.M. Miller, "Local Governments Offer Data to Software Tinkerers," www.nytimes.com/2009/12/07/technology/internet/07cities.html Accessed July 22, 2013, 2009.

Oakland Crimespotting, "The Pie of Time," http://blog.crimespotting.org/2009/06/the-pie-of-time Accessed July 22, 2013, 2009.

H. Schachter, "Reinventing Government or Reinventing Ourselves: Two Models for Improving Government Performance," *Public Administration Review* 55: 6 (1995) 530–537.

J.T. Shiller, "Preparing for Democracy How Community-Based Organizations Build Civic Engagement Among Urban Youth," *Urban Education* 48: 1 (2013) 69–91.

C. Shirky, *Cognitive Surplus: Creativity and Generosity in a Connected Age* (New York: Penguin Press, 2010).

C. Shirky and D. Pink, "Cognitive Surplus: The Great Spare-Time Revolution." http://www.wired.com/2010/05/ff_pink_shirky/ Accessed July 7, 2014, 2010.

K. Starbird, "Crowd Computation: Organizing Information During Mass Disruption Events," *Proceedings of the ACM 2012 Conference on Computer Supported Cooperative Work Companion*, 339–342, 2012.

A. Strauss and J.M. Corbin, *Grounded Theory in Practice* (Thousand Oaks, CA: SAGE Publications, Incorporated, 1997).

C.J. Tolbert and R.S. McNeal, "Unraveling the Effects of the Internet on Political Participation?," *Political Research Quarterly* 56: 2 (2003) 175–185.

UNFPA, "State of World Population 2007: Unleashing the Potential for Urban Growth" <http://www.unfpa.org/swp/2007presskit/pdf/sowp2007_eng.pdf> Accessed July 22, 2013.

Potential and Challenges for Social Media in the Neighborhood Context

Bonnie J. Johnson and Germaine R. Halegoua

ABSTRACT   *Many studies have focused on new media's role in connecting interest-based communities across vast geographic distances; fewer studies have examined how viable social media is as a communication tool within the neighborhood context. This study investigates the ways in which established modes of place-based neighborhood association, connection, and communication coincide or conflict with the perceived affordances of connection and association available in social networking sites. As a case study, we identified a neighborhood association that had seen its participation rates dwindle. The association's steering committee decided to turn to popular social media platforms (Facebook and Twitter) to revitalize. After the initial launch, they garnered only five "likes," three Twitter followers, and two members for the e-mail listserv out of a possible 550 households. A survey of neighborhood residents showed some potential for social media use but also significant mismatches between the perceived affordances of social media and residents' understanding of the place-based context and condition of the neighborhood. We found three main categories where perceptions and expectations of neighborhood communication did not mesh with social media affordances: perceived intimacy within the neighborhood; desired attributes of neighborhood communication; and expectations of digital and physical space and place.*

Introduction

Scholars have argued that many factors can unhinge people from "place" and neighborhoods. Suburbanization, mobility, attached garages, highway construction, the anonymity of cities, the telephone, television, and even refrigerators (Fischer, 1982; Olson, 1982; Silver, 1985; Rivlin, 1987; Hartley, 1999; Duany at al., 2000; Putnam, 2000) have been blamed for turning "neighbors" into "nigh-dwellers" (McClenahan, 1929). As seen in the list above, technology is a common culprit in the decline of neighborliness and sense of place. In terms of creating bonds between co-located people, it has been argued that social media and the Internet have had positive, negative, or complicated effects (Shah et al., 2001; Hampton and Wellman, 2003a, 2003b; Firmino, 2005; Kim et al., 2007; Evans-Cowley, 2010; Mandarano et al., 2010). Yet, after decades of researchers anticipating the end of the neighborhood, it adapts and "persists" (Olson, 1982: 493). Neighborhood organizing has always been challenging with failures commonplace. Nevertheless, neighborhood organizations have been successful by being flexible and meeting changing needs (Haeberle, 1986). Researchers have lamented that we do not know a great deal about the specific adaptive mechanisms, particularly in terms of communication, that neighborhood associations use to survive and thrive (Haeberle, 1986; Oropesa, 1995; Koschmann and Laster, 2011). As modes of everyday communication expand to include forms of digital media such as e-mail, web sites, blogs, and social networking sites, pertinent questions arise as to how neighborhoods and neighborhood associations are adapting and persisting in the digital age. This study examines how and whether the perceived affordances (Norman, 1988, 1999) of popular social networking sites (SNS), such as Facebook and Twitter, are compatible with "place" or what neighborhood associations and their residents desire and expect from neighborhood communication and relationships.

Social media appear to be a promising way for community organizers and neighbors to reach people quickly saving time, money, and the energy of volunteers (Kavanaugh et al., 2007; Kim et al., 2007). Research has shown that the use of information and communication technologies (ICTs) can lead to positive outcomes in terms of efficacy, levels of participation, and increased social capital. At the same time, they facilitate "portable personal communities" (Crump, 1977) exacerbating the shift from place-based communities to communities of interest divorced from place (Hillier, 2002). Other studies observe how social media connections are strongly dependent on and are supported by face-to-face contact (Takhteyev et al., 2012) and shared local contexts (Yardi and boyd, 2010). However, it is unclear whether the affordances of physical proximity and the expectations and desires of neighborhood association and neighborhood sociability mesh with the affordances of social media. We need further research on how and under what conditions the affordances of digital applications, such as social media, are compatible or incompatible with neighborhood contexts (Pinkett, 2003; Meredith et al., 2004; Evans-Cowley and Hollander, 2010).

Much of the literature from community informatics, urban planning, and communication studies has focused on the use of digital communication by planners, by neighbors seeking to rally support for or against particular projects, by students on university campuses, or by residents in specially "wired" neighborhoods (Hampton and Wellman, 1999; Ellison et al., 2006; Evans-Cowley, 2010; Evans-Cowley and Hollander, 2010). Many of these studies either do not deal with social media directly or do not address how a neighborhood association might best use social media that were implemented of their own accord. Additionally, there have been very few case studies of neighborhoods where social media or ICTs were not adopted with positive outcomes (Arnold et al., 2003). Although there is some understanding of why social media might not suit every neighborhood context (due to a lack of pre-existing social ties, community efficacy, or lack of digital skills), there is a scarcity of research analyzing the attitudes that might underlie the processes of the adoption or non-use of social media. Our study focuses on perceptions and ultimately the reluctance of neighborhood residents to use social media.

We found a neighborhood with an established identity but a neighborhood association that has seen its participation rates dwindle from hundreds to single digits. The association was considering dismantling after 38 years. Instead, the neighborhood's steering committee decided to turn to two social networking sites that they identified as the most popular and widely used, Facebook and Twitter, to build membership and disseminate information. The neighborhood association was particularly drawn to the notion that these forms of communication might reach a new and younger audience, and assumed that several neighborhood residents already used these sites. After the initial launch of a Facebook page and Twitter account, they gained no comments, responses, or retweets, and garnered only five "likes," three Twitter followers, and two members for the e-mail listserv out of a possible 550 households. We surveyed residents to investigate the reasons why they were not apt to join these social media networks. The survey focused on questions related to communication preferences, community efficacy, and constraints on neighborhood participation. Interestingly, respondents' written replies to a question about whether Facebook and/or Twitter are good tools for neighborhood communication revealed how perceptions of place, what neighborhood communication "ought to be," and the perceived norms and affordances of these social networking sites affected residents' views on the usefulness of Facebook and Twitter for neighborhood communication.

Social networking sites are conceptualized by boyd (2011: 39) as a distinct category of "networked publics ... (which) are publics that are restructured by networked technology." She notes that networked publics are similar to other "publics" in that they can serve social, cultural, and civic purposes and connect people to others outside their usual circles of friends and families. However, "the ways in which technology structures [networked publics] introduces distinct affordances that shape how people engage with these environments" (boyd, 2011: 39). She argues that the architecture or "bits-based nature of digital environments" construct unique forms of participation and interaction that differ from those in "atoms-based," physical environments. In this study we look at what happens when "bits-based" communication is introduced into a traditionally "atoms-based" environment and how the perceived affordances of social networking sites coincide with experiences and expectations of the neighborhood as a physical place and place-based community. We start with an overview of neighborhood and neighborhood associations in terms of place and how people interact in this context. We then review findings about the intersection of "bits-based" and "atoms-based" networks as digital communication is used within place-based communities. These sections are followed by descriptions of the case study and the research methods. The results reveal the mismatches between the neighborhood association and residents' perceptions of social media affordances and expectations and desires for neighborhood communication and interaction. Lastly limitations of the study, implications, and recommendations are addressed.

Neighborhood

Neighborhood and Place-Based Association

Researchers have questioned whether "place" matters for relationships and community in the digital age (Arnold, 2003) as "communities of interest" replace "communities of place" (Hillier, 2002). Hillier (2002: 51) maintains "it is only in the rare circumstances when people's interests and location overlap that localized community organizations establish and flourish." Certainly, "neighborhood" is "a social and geographic concept" (Coulton et al., 2012: 40) and highly susceptible to "subjective perceptions" as people define "their" neighborhoods (Martinez et al., 2002: 25). People have many relationships outside of their neighborhoods and technology makes those easier to maintain than ever. Kotler (1969: 9) explains, "The neighborhood was never a sufficient unit for friendship and social intercourse." However, Unger and Wandersman (1985: 141) maintain that "neighbors and neighborhoods still have a very important place in many individuals' lives... .The close spatial location of neighbors makes them unique to perform functions which other network members would find difficult" such as, occasional day care, borrowing tools, and lending help when needed (Warren, 1977).

Beyond social ties, "neighborhood" also can be defined as "a political settlement of small territory and familiar association, whose absolute property is its capacity for deliberative democracy" (Kotler, 1969: 2). Kotler sees an essential role for neighborhoods in being able to balance the power that can be exerted by a larger entity, namely the city. Certainly, neighborhood associations have been among the few entities to counterbalance business interests in US communities (Berry et al., 1993). Political roles of neighborhoods include organizing for public safety, protecting property values, or asking for infrastructure improvements (Warren, 1977). The term "neighborhood" connotes strong democratic values in the United States: solidarity, participation, and the heroics of common people (Looker, 2010).

"Neighborhood" also combines place and identity. Kotler (1969: 64–65) explains "[t]he most sensible way to locate the neighborhood is to ask people where it is" and "[a]bove all, the neighborhood has a name." A neighborhood's identity can reflect social status, traditions, and history (Warren, 1977). Some neighborhoods have the reputation of cultivating such strong interests and identities that their self-interests compete with the common good of the larger communities, but then there is the other extreme of disinterested and/or disenfranchised neighborhoods (McKenzie, 1922).

Individual, local, and neighborhood association characteristics can influence participation in neighborhood organizations. In a study of Seattle neighborhood associations Guest et al. (2006) found individual characteristics (homeownership, length of residence, having children) influenced neighboring ties more than any other local contexts. Additional studies verify that home ownership, length of residence, marital status, being older and/or retired, being middle class, and feeling positively about the neighborhood are generally associated with higher participation rates (Carr et al., 1976; Chaskin, 1997; Wandersman et al., 1987; Rainie et al., 2011). As far as local context is concerned, Guest et al. (2006) found in Seattle that older, established neighborhoods were more likely to be organized, but they clarified that having a particularly passionate person in the neighborhood or police attention was more likely to result in a neighborhood association than anything else. Similarly, in a study of neighborhoods in Calgary, researchers found that differences among neighborhood associations were explained more by the agency of the members than any factors (Davies and Townshend, 1994). Monti and colleagues (2003) track changes in social ties and civic engagement from 1974 to 1994 and find that fears about vast declines in civicness have been overblown. They note, "[t]he civic bubble we live in... can change shape without doing us any great harm" as people learn different ways to be involved

(Monti et al., 2003: 159). This harkens back to notions of adaptability and understanding how neighborhood associations are adjusting over time and whether newer, digital forms of communication are helpful or not. Social media users are more likely to participate in neighborhood associations (Rainie et al., 2011), but does that mean social media works for neighborhood communication?

Neighborhood and Digital Communication

Although technologies like the Internet and mobile phones aid communication across vast geographic distances, they have been found to enhance local relationships as well (Wellman, 1999; Wellman and Hampton, 1999, 2003; Hampton and Wellman, 2003b). Studies of community networks find that ICTs are often employed as ways to enhance opportunities for face to face interactions (Hollan and Stornetta, 1992; Hampton and Wellman, 1999; Cooperrider and Avital, 2004; Carroll, 2012). Pigg and Crank (2004) suggest that the use of ICTs within place-based communities can extend social networks, provide access to resources and information for action or mobilization, and enhance solidarity, trust, and reciprocity. In terms of social networking sites, such as Facebook, Ellison et al. (2006) found SNS could enhance place-based communities through combining offline and online interactions, with positive connections between bridging social capital and maintained social capital between people who transition from one offline community to another (Ellison et al., 2007). danah boyd (2011) has noted that certain architectural features of social networking sites such as streams of user-generated content, individual profiles, and status updates, Friends lists and publicly articulated connections, and public commenting tools as well as technological affordances of digital media (persistence, replicability, scalability, and searchability) shape the structure of networked publics as well as practices and people's participation within them. boyd (2011) also notes that these affordances lead to certain dynamics: invisible audiences, collapsed contexts, and the blurring of public and private, that members of social networking sites grapple with and that shape their experiences, social interactions, and possibly their perceptions of or concerns about these sites.

Studies show that ICT networks are used for local social capital building activities (Wellman et al., 2001; Kavanaugh and Patterson, 2002), and that wired residents generally have more neighborhood connections than non-wired residents (Hampton, 2003). In terms of how digital media affordances and platforms shape neighborhood political participation, Hampton (2003, 2007) found that weak ties are primarily enriched from ICT use within neighborhoods, and that ICTs such as e-mail, forums, and listservs help to create large, dense networks of weak ties that facilitate collective action. Several researchers have argued that neighborhoods with ICTs are better equipped to address local concerns (Schuler, 1996; Carroll, 2012). Pattavina et al. (2002) illustrate how gathering and archiving neighborhood-level crime data can build local knowledge and better understandings of crime and crime prevention. In their study of Netville, Hampton and Wellman (2003a, 2003b) found information flows were improved inexpensively (in terms of time, cost, effort), and that listservs and forums created a new visibility for networks of action. However, during moments of stability, when Netville was not dealing with a crisis, activity on the neighborhood message boards and e-mail lists decreased.

Nevertheless, it seems that a minority of residents in the United States engage with neighbors or neighborhood associations via digital technologies. A national survey conducted by Pew in 2009 ("Neighbors Online") found that face-to-face and phone calls were the most common methods of communicating with neighbors. While participants surveyed by Pew used a range of approaches to communicate with neighbors, approximately one in five Americans used digital tools (e-mail and mailing lists, social media, blogs, and web sites) to communicate with neighbors and monitor community developments (Smith, 2010). The Pew study (2010) also found that e-mail was the most common digital means of communication between neighbors. E-mail use was most common among people 65 and older, followed by 30–49 and 50–64 age ranges respectively, with more parents than non-parents reaching out to neighbors via e-mail. The lowest rate of e-mail between neighbors was among 18–29 year-olds. SNS were most common among 18–29 and 30–49 year olds (both age ranges were equally likely to use SNS), half as much at 50+. Other than age, there was little variation. However, only a small percentage (~14 percent) of all SNS users, used social media to communicate with neighbors. The research is consistent in being encouraged by the potential of ICTs to foster connections online and offline, but the encouragement is contingent on context and platform. Above all, there is an agreement among scholars that it is difficult for social media to create ties where there are none already.

Findings from community informatics studies are tempered with both opportunities and risks associated with community networking (Schuler, 1996; Gurstein, 2004; Carroll, 2012). However, this literature generally begins with the perspective that communities can be "empowered" by ICTs if these technologies are designed in accordance with pre-existing cultures, norms, and logics of particular communities, and if residents and communities become authors as well as audiences (Gurstein, 2004: 2). Importantly, researchers note that access to ICTs will not automatically create or incubate social networks where none previously existed (Hampton and Wellman, 2003a, 2003b; Foth, 2006a, 2006b; Gaved and Foth, 2006). Interestingly, Hampton et al. (2011b) found that place-based relationships have slightly less resonance for social media users, which might be linked to previous findings (Hampton, 2007) that residents with few neighborhood ties are more likely to use social media in their daily lives (Hampton et al., 2011b: 1046), or that these social media users might also be highly mobile and use ICTs as a primary means of connecting with others (Ames et al., 2011). Therefore, social media use within place-based communities has been shown to strengthen pre-existing ties, but has also been shown to be a common characteristic among those lacking ties with fellow local residents. These contradictions imply that there may be a disconnect between perceived affordances of the neighborhood as a place or social context, residents' communication preferences within these environments, and the technological affordances and central dynamics of social media that requires further research.

Background and Case Study: Indian Hills Neighborhood and Social Media Presence

The neighborhood chosen for this case study is "Indian Hills" and its neighborhood association is the Indian Hills Neighborhood Association (IHNA). This

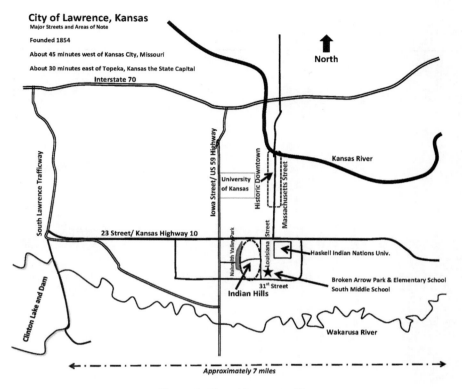

Figure 1: City of Lawrence, Kansas.

neighborhood is located in the city of Lawrence, Kansas (See Figures 1 and 2), which has a population of 87,643 (See Table 1). In the 1950s, the neighborhood was one of the first expansions of the city in a southerly direction (IHNA, 2003). The neighborhood is composed of mostly single-family homes with a sprinkling of duplex and triplex apartments.

The IHNA was organized in 1974 to oppose a proposal to build an apartment complex in a nearby floodplain. It began with a group of neighbors on Arkansas Street next to Naismith Valley Park and then expanded. In the past, IHNA regularly mailed newsletters to 550 households and as late as 2003 had 150 dues-paying members (IHNA, 2003). IHNA was one of the founding members of the Lawrence Association of Neighborhoods (LAN), which is an umbrella organization of Lawrence neighborhood associations. LAN was organized in 1987 in order to create a coalition able to counteract what was seen at the time as an overly influential development community within Lawrence (Lopes, 2001).

Until 2010, IHNA collected annual dues or donations and held elections of officers and a steering committee. After seeing participation rates tumble and being unable to muster volunteers, in February 2012, the remaining members of the steering committee and officers (five residents) met to determine whether the organization should disband. At that meeting, the last elected Chair of IHNA (the lead author of this article) proposed an experiment to see whether social media could turn around the failing neighborhood association, and the committee agreed to try. Members of the committee were willing to try something

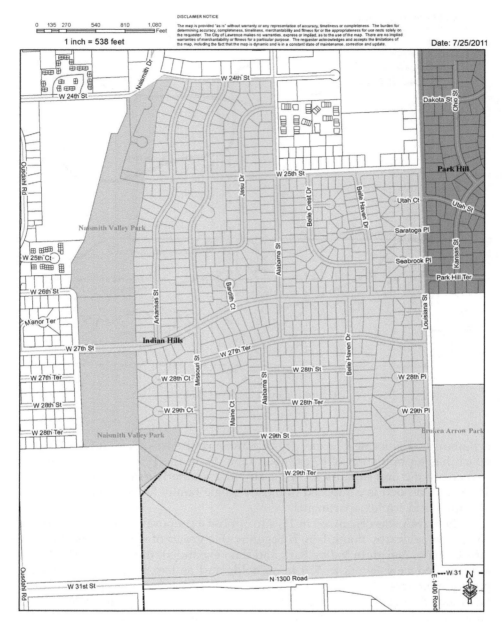

Figure 2: The boundaries of the Indian Hills neighborhood.
Source: City of Lawrence, Kansas, Planning and Development Service Department.

different (other than newsletters, meetings, and door hangers), and to somehow reach younger, newer residents.

Facebook and Twitter were selected by the IHNA, in particular, because committee members had heard about the popularity of these social media outlets. The committee members assumed Facebook and Twitter would be what residents already used, and they did not have any experience with or knowledge of other digital media or social media options. The committee's perceived affordances of

Table 1: Demographic comparison of the United States, Lawrence, and Indian Hills.

	United States	Lawrence	Indian Hills
Population	308,745,538	87,643	1,527
Female	51%	50%	51%
Male	49%	50%	49%
Age			
Under 18	24%	18%	23%
65 or over	13%	8%	15%
Race			
American Indian, Alaskan Native, Native Hawaiian, Pacific Islander	1%	3%	3%
Asian	5%	5%	1%
African American	13%	5%	4%
Some other race	6%	2%	1%
Two or more races	3%	4%	5%
White	72%	82%	85%
Ethnicity			
Hispanic	16%	6%	5%
Households			
Average Household Size	2.58	2.28	2.43
Occupied Housing Units	89%	93%	96%
Owner Occupied Units	65%	47%	69%
Renter Occupied Units	35%	53%	31%

Note: Percentages may not add up to 100 due to rounding.
Source: 2010 *US Census (2013)*.

Facebook and Twitter were that they were inexpensive, required minimal time commitment on the part of the producer and consumer of information, had an immediate and wide reach, and were easy to use. Although social networking sites afford users the ability to generate content, IHNA recognized Facebook and Twitter in terms of a broadcasting model, pushing content to neighborhood "listeners," who could ask questions in response to a post or message, but could not create announcements or posts themselves. They also did not think about users being able to see each other's profiles. It is important to note that the IHNA steering committee created a Facebook Page—a Facebook profile that puts more authorial control in the hands of the creator of the account, is "designed to be the official profiles for entities, such as celebrities, brands or businesses" and is public by default (Pineda, 2010: paragraph 8)–rather than a Facebook Group—designed for small group communication. It "allows people to come together around a common cause, issue, or activity; to organize, express objectives, discuss issues, post photos and share related content" (Pineda, 2010: paragraph 8)—mainly because they were not aware of the "group" option.

Social media researchers have struggled with how to evaluate digital communication platforms and services within a fast-paced, ever changing technological context (Ellison and boyd, 2013). However, the focus on Facebook and Twitter in this study may be useful in that they rely on certain SNS tools and affordances that continue to be relevant over time and between sites; for example: individual profiles, visibility of social networks, user-generated content, commenting, and stream-based updates. IHNA's Facebook page and Twitter account went live on May 6, 2012 and remain online today. On May 11, e-mails were sent to the 16 residents who had been active in the past, inviting them to "like" the Facebook page and/or to "follow" IHNA on Twitter. This e-mail generated three "likes" on Facebook and two Twitter followers. Between May 13–16, 550 door hangers were delivered to households in the neighborhood announcing the Facebook page, Twitter account, and e-mail address where residents could sign up to be on an e-mail list. The door hanger also announced the remaining annual event that still generates interest, the Neighborhood Garage Sale Day that set for June 2, 2012. The door hangers generated two more "likes" on Facebook and one additional Twitter follower and two requests to be added to the e-mail list. All of this activity occurred from May 11 to May 18, 2012. In comparison, 23 households participated in the garage sale day.

The first version of the Facebook page utilized the standard template. It had a photo of the entry sign to the Indian Hills subdivision, a neighborhood map, and basic information. From July to September 2012, more photos from the 2010 IHNA potluck and history of the neighborhood were added. A neighborhood meeting was announced in September via Facebook, Twitter, and an e-mail was sent to the usual 16 e-mail participants plus two new participants. Seven people attended the September 25, 2012 meeting, but none were new members. In January 2013, a survey was mailed to neighborhood residents to assess why the social media outreach had not been more effective. Soon after the survey was sent out, two additional residents "liked" the Facebook page in February and April 2013, but the Twitter feed gained no new followers.

Methods

The Indian Hills neighborhood was chosen for this case study because of the lead author's involvement in the IHNA, allowing her to be a participant observer, but more importantly it was chosen because of the unique situation presented by a neighborhood association facing the critical decision of carrying on with the usual methods of neighborhood involvement and dying or adapting and experimenting with popular social media platforms and, hopefully, surviving. Conveniently, the neighborhood is similar to overall US demographics in terms of age, household size, and renter/owner occupied units (See Table 1).

On January 24, 2013 a questionnaire with a self-addressed stamped envelope was mailed to each of the 573 households in Indian Hills. Three were returned due to vacancies. Upon analyzing the neighborhood boundaries, 23 more households were found than the usual 550 on the IHNA mailing list. To help boost return rates, a postcard was mailed on January 3, 2013 informing residents that a survey would arrive shortly (Dillman, 2000). Out of 570 valid addresses, 212 surveys were returned for a return rate of 37 percent. The survey questions asked respondents demographic information, length of residency, their sense of neighborhood belonging, neighborhood boundaries, neighborhood name, any local issues, their civic participation, and how they would prefer to communicate with the neighborhood (if they wanted to communicate). The survey used and modified questions from previous studies on sense of community and community participation (Glynn, 1981; Chavis and Wandersman, 1990; Saguaro Seminar, 2000; Sigmon, et al., 2002; Martinez et al., 2002; Perkins and Long, 2002; Hampton et al., 2011a; Coulton et al., 2012). Surveys were anonymous unless contact information was provided in order to be contacted later on for an interview.

For this study, understanding why neighbors were not apt to use the social media outlets offered by the neighborhood association was of most interest. As a result, the bulk of the analysis is based on responses to the open ended question, "Do you think Facebook and/or Twitter are good ways to communicate with the neighborhood? Why/why not?" The analysis consists of open and axial coding of the responses from which key themes were identified and used to analyze the data (Strauss and Corbin, 1990, 1998; Cresswell 2007). The rest of the analysis looks for any differences (using t tests) in the residents who thought social media was a good form of neighborhood communication and those who did not. These results are organized along the lines of similar research looking for the influence of individual, local, and neighborhood association characteristics on neighboring ties and neighborhood organization participation rates. Other survey results are reported as percentages.

Results

The ages of those who responded to the survey ranged from 20 to 91 with a mean of 58 and standard deviation of 17 ($n = 199$). Fifty-nine percent were employed and 30 percent were retired ($n = 211$). Length of residency goes from a few months up to 55 years and a mean of 19 years (sd $= 15$, $n = 211$). The majority (59 percent) think they will be in the neighborhood for at least five more years, but 26 percent "Don't know" if they will or not ($n = 212$). The overwhelming majority own their own single-family home (96 percent, $n = 212$) and the other 4 percent rent and live in half of a duplex. Twenty-four percent out of 212 have children in the home under 18. Seventy percent of respondents ($n = 212$) have bachelor's degrees or above. Lastly, 86 percent ($n = 212$) spend an hour or more on the Internet or e-mail (outside of work) in a typical week. The majority of respondents are well educated and are online.

In terms of how people identify and define "neighborhood," when asked, "What is the name of your neighborhood?" an overwhelming 86 percent of 206 people wrote in "Indian Hills." Only 18 respondents marked "I don't know." The questionnaire also asked respondents to identify, "What area do you define as your neighborhood?" The choices and associated percentage of responses are as follows:

- The 2 or 3 houses immediately adjacent to my house. (5 percent out of 205)
- The 5 to 10 houses next to my house and immediately across the street. (18 percent)
- The 20 or so houses on my street and nearby streets. (26 percent)
- The houses within the Indian Hills Neighborhood Association area. (26 percent)
- The houses in the Broken Arrow Elementary School Area. (19 percent)
- Other (please specify). (2 percent)

Who Would Use Social Media in the Neighborhood?

Respondents were asked if they knew that IHNA had a Facebook page and a Twitter feed. For Facebook, 9 percent ($n = 212$) marked "yes" and for knowledge of the Twitter feed, 3 percent ($n = 212$) marked "yes." The survey then asked people to pick the three best ways for "the neighborhood to communicate with you." Below are the choices and associated percentages from most chosen to least:

- Mail (69 percent, $n = 212$)
- E-mail (51 percent)
- Door hangers (41 percent)
- Telephone (25 percent)
- Facebook (20 percent)
- Word of mouth (19 percent)
- Website (14 percent)
- Google+ (3 percent)
- Twitter (1 percent)
- Blog (1 percent)
- Mobile App (1 percent)
- MySpace (0 percent)
- LinkedIn (0 percent)

We then combined those who chose at least one of the following: Facebook, Twitter, and Google+ as preferred means of neighborhood communication into a group and compared this group to those who did not choose a social media option. This group is called the "Social Media Group" in Table 2 (See Table 2). We looked for any differences in terms of individual, local, and neighborhood association characteristics. In the table, for the "size of neighborhood" this is where people were asked to define the boundaries of the neighborhood going from the two or three houses next to them on up to the catchment area for the Broken Arrow Elementary School which is much larger than the Indian Hills neighborhood (range from 1 to 5). The statements in the table in quotes are items where respondents were asked to give their level of agreement from 1 to 5 with 5 being the most agreement. The Civic Participation measure is an additive scale ranging from 0 to 6, where respondents received one point for every one of the following they did in the last year: signed a petition, voted in a local election, worked on a community project, attended a political meeting or rally, voted in the US presidential election, donated blood, or participated in any demonstration, protest, boycott, or march. The question about knowing people's names who live on one's block offered choices from 1 to 5 with 1 being "none" and 5 being "almost everyone."

From Table 2, it is apparent that the Social Media Group members are younger, have children, and are newer to the neighborhood (individual characteristics). They identify with a larger area of the neighborhood which may mean that they identify with the Broken Arrow school catchment area because of their children and their children's friends. As newcomers, they would like to know more about how to begin to be involved with the neighborhood association. Even though they are slightly more in agreement with some of the reasons for not being involved with the neighborhood association (child care and work) than the non-social media group, their mean scores are still in the range of disagreement with these items. Both groups are similar in that there is slight agreement that they would be more involved if not for obligations to other groups. What is striking is the social media group consists of people who participate in civic life and want a neighborhood association and consider it important. In terms of neighborhood ties and opinions about the neighborhood association, there is no difference between the groups in terms of knowing neighbors by name or in trusting the

Table 2: Differences between those choosing social media tools and those who did not.

	Social Media Group Member?		
	No (mean)	Yes (mean)	t test
Individual Characteristics			
Age	61	47	$t(197) = -5.80^{***}$
Children under 18 (range from 0 to 6)	0.35	0.88	$t(210) = 2.66^{**}$
Length of residency (years)	21	12	$t(209) = -5.01^{***}$
"I use the internet to connect with my neighborhood."	1.77	2.13	$t(195) = 2.13^{**}$
"In an ideal neighborhood, no one would take any interest in what I am doing."	2.11	1.86	$t(204) = -1.81^{*}$
"I would be more involved with my neighborhood if I ...			
- had a more flexible work schedule."	2.49	2.88	$t(198) = 2.08^{**}$
- had adequate childcare."	1.88	2.32	$t(192) = 2.82^{**}$
- felt more welcome."	2.36	2.79	$t(202) = 2.40^{**}$
- knew how to begin."	2.61	3.18	$t(200) = 3.12^{**}$
- had fewer obligations to other organizations."	2.64	2.84	$t(202) = 1.01$
Civic participation	2.61	3.06	$t(210) = 2.33^{**}$
"Thinking about the people who live on your block or cul-de-sac: How many people do you know by name?"	3.68	3.63	$t(205) = -0.26$
Neighborhood Association Characteristics/Preferences			
Size of Neighborhood	3.29	3.72	$t(199) = 2.53^{**}$
"An ideal neighborhood has an active neighborhood organization."	3.60	3.80	$t(207) = 1.69^{*}$
"My neighborhood should have a neighborhood organization."	3.59	4.00	$t(200) = 3.03^{**}$
"I can trust IHNA to do what is right."	3.32	3.27	$t(206) = -0.45$
Local Characteristics			
"Living in Lawrence gives me a sense of belonging to a community."	3.80	4.06	$t(202) = 1.76^{*}$
"The City of Lawrence government is run for the benefit of all the people."	2.80	3.14	$t(208) = 1.92^{*}$

***p value $< .001$.
**p value $< .05$.
*p value $< .10$.

IHNA (neighborhood association characteristics). It is notable that the social media group members identify with Lawrence more and are more trusting of the City of Lawrence (local characteristics). Those who have lived in the neighborhood longer may be showing some weariness from past conflict with "City Hall and/or developers."

Studies of digital media use within neighborhoods have shown that younger, well educated, higher income populations are more apt to use online platforms like e-mail, listservs, and discussion forums to communicate with neighbors (Smith, 2010; Arnold et al., 2003). Additionally, parents and younger residents have been more likely to use digital tools for neighborhood communication or to sign up for local e-mail or mobile alerts (Smith, 2010). Researchers have also found that Facebook users are more trusting than non-users (Hampton et al., 2011a). Therefore, based on individual characteristics and attitudes about the local context and neighborhood association, it seems likely that at least some of the Indian Hills residents would have opted-in to the social media sites created by the steering committee. However, this was not the case either after the initial door hanger or the survey. The following section discusses our findings related to social media use or non-use within the Indian Hills neighborhood.

Is Social Media a Good Way to Communicate with the Neighborhood?

When asked whether social media such as Facebook and Twitter in particular were good ways to communicate with the neighborhood, survey participants indicated various responses. The meaning of the term "neighborhood" in these questions was left for respondents to interpret. However, in the write-in portion of the question, several respondents indicated who in particular they would like to communicate with over social media, what defines their neighborhood, and under what conditions and contexts social media were understood to be positive, negative, or potential ways of communicating. Overall, the responses to the open-ended question, "Do you think Facebook and/or Twitter are good ways to communicate with the neighborhood? Why/why not?" were coded into four categories with their associated percentages: Yes (25 percent), No (41 percent), Maybe (13 percent), and Don't know/not sure (4 percent) ($n = 177$).

Some respondents considered using social media to be a meaningful way to communicate and their comments are included here in quotes. People who said "Yes" without qualification noted that social media were convenient, cost effective, not labor intensive, "easy" ways to stay connected and receive up-to-date information, and allowed for "instant" or "immediate" communication. A related (and rather sizable) category of respondents were participants who noted social media use within the neighborhood as potentially beneficial if used under the proper conditions. A common concern among these respondents was that even if a neighborhood Facebook or Twitter page existed, there is no guarantee that members of the community would be able to find it, or would be aware of the neighborhood's social media presence. Additionally, these participants cautioned that if the neighborhood association used Facebook or Twitter to communicate, then it would have to be done "correctly," meaning that it would have to be regularly updated, full of interesting and relevant content, have a base of active participants who were invested in the site, and "season it with an occasional dash of indesputible [sic] humor."

Social Media as Unequal, Limiting, or Undesirable

However, the majority of residents surveyed were hesitant about, or preferred not to use social media for neighborhood communication. Several respondents mentioned unequal access to social media and the exclusion of some people from neighborhood communication as key reasons why services like Facebook and Twitter were not good ways to communicate with the neighborhood. This trope of exclusion, inequality, and "convenient for some but not all" was reiterated using many different factors in order to support these claims. Respondents cited lack of digital skills, lack of skills needed to use social media specifically, lack of access to a computer, and lack of access to an Internet connection as conditions that might promote exclusion from neighborhood communication. Aside from digital literacy and/or digital access, some explanations for conditions of inclusion or exclusion were that fellow residents: might not be familiar with social media, are not interested in using or prefer not to use social networking sites, or do not have accounts. For example a reiterated response was, "No, not everyone owning a house in this neighborhood uses Facebook or Twitter and you would be leaving them out."

Several respondents mentioned that social media within the neighborhood might be a good secondary or supplemental source of information and communication, but would be insufficient if social networking sites were the primary form of communication. The concern that social media would overtake all other forms of neighborhood communication was a common fear among participants. Although our survey did not indicate or imply that social media would displace face-to-face meetings, events, newsletters, door hangers, or any other pre-existing mode of communication, residents concluded that the presence of social media would eclipse other modes of communication and voiced discontent with this perceived future. For example, many residents shared the perspective: "I don't rely on electronic contacts—they are only effective if everyone can and will use them. Those who don't, don't communicate if that is the only option." Or as another resident noted: "They [Facebook and Twitter] are limited forms of communication because not all people choose to use Facebook and/or Twitter. Other forms of communication probably would be superior." In some cases, respondents emphatically represented themselves as one of the residents who would be excluded by a shift to neighborhood communication via social media: "[Social media would] Probably [be a good way to communicate] if people know about it. But not everyone has a computer or belongs to facebook or tweets. *I don't*."

The most common hesitation or complaint about unequal access to social media for neighborhood communication was articulated through a discussion of age and life stage. Respondents tended to equate mature age with decreased knowledge and/or desire to use social media (or digital technologies in general). Residents identified themselves as old, retired, or ill and offered these conditions as reasons for not using computers or social media. For yes, no, maybe, and I don't know answers, the age of participants was frequently mentioned as a reason either to use (because you or other residents were young) or not to use (because you or other residents were old) social media. The mean age of the "Yes" respondents was 50, the "No" respondents' mean age was 63, while the means from the "Maybes" and "Don't knows" were 56 and 72 respectively.

Additionally, participants in the study often linked social media and digital media to youth and analog forms of media to elderly populations. Repeated sentiments among residents included:

- "It [social media] can be a good source of information except we have older neighbors that are not on the computer so they are left out. Neighborhood newsletters [*sic*] were more helpful."
- "I do not use facebook or twitter. I think mailing flyers is the best way. Many in our neighborhood are retired, online may not be utilized as often."
- "Yes, for younger people. I think that older residents would still need to get a phone call or something in the mail."
- "Many older folks don't use Facebook and/or twitter."
- "The older people in the IHNA (me included) may not use these."

- "Facebook and Twitter are the modern way of communicating among various people and organizations. However, older people (over 65) might not use the online method."
- "No - old people don't use the internet."

In some cases people noted their age, life stage, or physical condition as a reason they were not able to assess or answer the write-in question:

- "Infirmities (sic) limit my ability to evaluate this."
- "Age limits my ability to evaluate this."
- "In general yes (social media would be a good way to communicate), but we are retired and ill, so no."

Social Media as Inadequate for Neighborhood Communication

Factors such as the perceived size and scale of the neighborhood and the number of residents an individual did not already know were referenced as reasons to avoid social media for neighborhood communication or social networking. A few residents noted that they only use social media, such as Facebook, to communicate with people they already knew or already had ties with. These residents noted that the Indian Hills neighborhood did not feel like a close knit group; therefore they would not want to use Facebook in order to communicate with the neighborhood.

Representative responses include:

- "No, I personally limit facebook to a limited close group. Any other use is an intrusion on my space. Ie, not signed onto facebook for any company or commercial companies . . . "
- "If the neighborhood felt smaller and safer I'd say facebook. But I don't feel comfortable having people in the neighborhood see my facebook. It is too big to feel like a tight knit neighborhood."

Some residents noted that they would use Facebook to communicate with neighbors who they already knew, and some residents noted that they already use Facebook to communicate with neighbors in their social networks/circles.

A few participants mentioned that social media was a tool to communicate with people in geographically distant locations and not those who lived in geographic proximity. Several participants shared this perspective regarding social media: "Not really, because 'neighborhood' is so associated w/ *physical* space." Additionally, these participants noted that neighborhood associations and neighbors should take advantage of shared geographic proximity in order to connect. Events and face-to-face contact were seen as "places," moments, or sites through which the neighborhood should communicate and connect. For example, one respondent suggested using Facebook "to contact those who live far away or that one might never/rarely see or talk to if not for Facebook. Neighborhoods should have in-person contact or fun events to attend for people to get to know one another."

The small size of the neighborhood and its physicality were read as reasons to question the neighborhood use of social media and to support analog forms of communication that required walking around the neighborhood, delivering information door to door or face to face. For example, one resident noted: "Yes & No.

As a small geographical area, flyers would be more effective at reaching people who don't already know the other people in the area, or who don't have access to the Internet."

One respondent noted that they associate "FB [Facebook] with 'nonwork' or leisure" and would prefer e-mail as a way to communicate about neighborhood issues. It is unclear which category the neighborhood fits into, but for this respondent, the neighborhood is somehow related to "work" and not entirely in the realm of leisure. Therefore, Facebook was not read as an appropriate tool to communicate with the neighborhood. Perhaps a more socially focused neighborhood association would fit into the "leisure" category but a more politically focused neighborhood association fits under "work." The categorization and understanding of the roles of neighborhood associations and the meaning of neighborhoods as varying from more social or more political is something to be investigated further during the forthcoming interviews.

General Complaints about Social Media

Residents also voiced complaints or displeasure about using social media in general. Common observances and/or complaints were that social media were impersonal (especially as compared to face-to-face communication), a waste of time, intrusive, annoying, or something individual residents were "not into." A few respondents mentioned that they were already "super-saturated" or overwhelmed with Facebook pages and requests. In this vein, one resident mentioned that: "Maybe—only if important updates are posted. If I were to get constant e-mails about posts/updates I would probably not take them seriously. . ."

Privacy concerns were also mentioned, albeit infrequently. One respondent who noted privacy concerns directly did not specify exactly what these concerns were. However, this resident noted that they would prefer e-mail as a mode of communication. In addition, a few people mentioned control issues as a reason to avoid services like Facebook: "Facebook decides what messages are delivered and there is not 100 percent participation in either. I think e-mail would better." "I have a facebook page but only for receiving some info. I dislike the unfiltered access social media provide for sharing all kinds of communication." Instead of social media, participants noted that they preferred a web page, newsletters, face-to-face encounters, "fun events," e-mail, mailing flyers, pamphlets, brochures, and posting signs around the neighborhood as preferable means of communication.

Discussion

Based on this study, there is potential and limits for neighborhoods and neighborhood associations seeking to use social media to connect neighbors and boost participation. One limitation is that social media alone are not sufficient to "jumpstart" a neighborhood organization. It is quick, easy, and inexpensive for neighborhood organizers to use, but if no one is there to network with, the effort is wasted. Interestingly, certain perceptions of the affordances and norms of social media platforms such as Facebook and Twitter were understood by neighborhood residents to be in conflict with expectations, desires, and perceived affordances of neighborhood communication.

The potential is that there is a small group of people, the Social Media Group (23 percent in our sample of 212) who would use Facebook, Google+, and/or Twitter to communicate with the neighborhood, and it turns out these are exactly the kinds of people who would benefit a neighborhood organization and neighborhood network the most. Members of the Social Media Group in this study tend to identify with a larger neighborhood area (not just their immediate neighbors). Previous research shows that people with more expansive views of "neighborhood" are more engaged neighbors (Coulton et al., 2012). For our study, the Social Media Group consists of newer residents with children. Perkins and Long (2002) indicate that young families are good investments for neighborhood organizations because the parents can become good neighborhood organization volunteers later on when they are older and their children move away. Children are where "place" and "interests" intersect as parents look for a neighborhood where their children can safely play and there are neighbors nearby who keep watch (Martinez et al., 2002). Also, as newer residents, the Social Media Group seems more trusting of the City of Lawrence and thus perhaps more optimistic about interacting politically as a neighborhood group. Successful neighborhood organizations have members who feel they have "power" within the larger community (Speer et al., 1995). Plus, even though these are newer residents they are still aware that their neighborhood is called "Indian Hills". The potential benefit of social media use for neighborhood associations is further discussed in another paper (Johnson and Halegoua, 2013), where we identify and analyze the potential in reaching out to those who would like to use social media to communicate with their neighbors and neighborhood association. We are currently conducting interviews with neighborhood residents in order to better understand the ways in which the perceived affordances of social media mesh with perceived affordances of neighborhood connection and communication. However, in this paper we will focus on the "mismatches" between the perceived affordance of social media and the neighborhood context.

In our study we asked: "Why didn't residents of the Indian Hills neighborhood join and connect with each other using the social media networks set up by the neighborhood association?" Other than general complaints, personal preferences against the use of social media, or the self-reported lack of computer access, Internet access, or digital skills, we found three main categories that were reiterated by residents in order to explain their lack of social media use within the community and that imply mismatches between the perceived affordances of social media and neighborhood context and communication: lack of perceived intimacy within the neighborhood; desired attributes of neighborhood communication; and expectations of digital and physical space and place.

Lack of Perceived Intimacy within the Neighborhood

The lack of perceived intimacy within the neighborhood emphasizes that the relationships and information shared on Facebook are more personal or intimate than would be shared with "neighbors" who were not also already friends. Propinquity does not, by itself, create a tie strong enough for access to online profiles that display social ties and networks, status updates, and personal information (see Wellman et al., 1988). By imagining the affordances of social networking sites strictly in terms of communication (posting information, commenting, and stream-based updates) the IHNA Steering Committee did not think of the access to profiles and whether people would be comfortable having "ties" to people they did not know. This points to the use of Facebook specifically and indicates that perhaps a more "impersonal" online networking tool might be more appropriate. According to our findings, e-mail or a service that resembles a listserv, discussion forum, or messaging system that allows for minimal profile creation and no or low visibility of social ties might be used as a valuable tool for neighborhood communication, especially in neighborhoods where the neighborhood associations play more of a political than social role.

Desired Attributes of Neighborhood Communication

Our findings show that there is a perception that neighborhood communication and participation should be egalitarian and inclusive (democratic). A neighborhood organization that relies on social media alone not only risks falling victim to digital divides and exclusion but also risks alienating social media users who would feel like the organization was not inclusive and fair to all. There was hesitation or resistance to social media use among respondents (those who were tech-savvy and those who were not) because they saw such platforms as privileged among youth, the tech savvy, people who owned a computer, and those who knew how to use social media. The perception that not all neighborhood members could access social media was a major concern for the majority of the participants in the study. On a related note, respondents were concerned that social media would become the only communication tool used by the neighborhood association and thus would leave people out.

There seemed to be a perception among study participants that a significant portion of the Indian Hills Neighborhood were elderly (indicated by the significant number of comments about age). There was also a shared perception that increased age negatively influences social media access and desire or ability to use digital technologies. These comments might indicate a concern about the lack of participation and/or people to talk to if the neighborhood used social media. If participants thought that neighborhood communication should be egalitarian and open to all members, then these social media networks might be read as overly homogenous due to age-based exclusivity and not representative of what neighborhood communication "ought to be."

Expectations of Digital and Physical Space

A common perception among residents of Indian Hills was that social media did not mesh with the space and place of the neighborhood. Residents commented on geographic propinquity and the scale of the neighborhood as reasons why the use of social media by the neighborhood association seemed curious or inappropriate. Respondents also returned to the idea that neighborhoods were about meeting face-to-face. Therefore, the neighborhood organization needed to utilize the context of the community and have events or activities where people could interact face-to-face. For those in the Social Media Group as well as non-users, the combination of face to face events and online communication might prove particularly meaningful. This echoes some of Arnold et al.'s (2003) study on a neighborhood intranet. The researchers noted that, ironically, residents tended to frequent face-to-face events about the development of online forums more frequently than the online forums themselves. If members of the Social Media Group are targeted as potential leaders or members of a neighborhood association, the combination of face-to-face and online communication and activities should prove beneficial in promoting participation and neighborhood efficacy. Social networking sites are not a "shortcut" to creating ties or a substitute for neighborhood leaders going door to door and meeting people.

Limitations of this Study

This study is of one neighborhood in one city and, as such, might not be generalizable to a larger population. Future studies can go further in disentangling which factors (individual, local, neighborhood association, and communication medium affordances) affect the success or failure of neighborhood associations' use of social networking sites. However, as a case study testing the potential of social media to aid a struggling neighborhood organization, it offers useful findings and sheds light on perceptions of social media within a neighborhood context.

Gaved and Foth (2006) offer some suggestions for creating sustainable, digital social networks: cultivate and maintain a sense of ownership of the network; simple, open-ended tools are the most successful; the network should be a top-down and bottom-up hybrid; develop internal and/or external outlets for technical training and support. Drawing on these suggestions, the IHNA steering committee could have worked to cultivate a sense of ownership of these networks by working with committee members in the creation of the social media accounts and pages. Our results indicate that outlets for training and support in social media and computer use may have been helpful for some residents. Additionally, this study was conducted nine months after the creation of the IHNA Facebook and Twitter accounts. A delay in the study could have allowed for more advertising and promotion of the site and potentially an increased number of online participants.

Conclusion

In light of the recent surge in mobile applications and social networking sites dedicated to neighborhood communication and/or place-based communities such as Next Door, Everyblock, Locally, Neighbor Tree, Neighbor.ly, i-Neighbors, Neighborland, and Home Elephant (to name a few) we feel that research into the use and perceptions of affordances and norms of social media within a neighborhood is particularly timely. While community planners have found some success using social media, digital games, and online tools for participatory planning and education, questions remain about the use of these tools for neighborhood communication, neighborhood engagement, and use by neighborhood associations. While some residents identified that the use of social networking sites, particularly Facebook, would be beneficial to their neighborhood communication, access to information, and participation, we found some mismatches or conflicts between the perceived affordances of social media and the neighborhood context.

Physical place and online space interface and interact in nuanced and complex ways. We find that certain people are apt to experiment with or use social media to communicate with neighbors about neighborhood news and events, but we also find that there are various hesitations about using social media within the neighborhood context that are worthy of further exploration and consideration. The perspectives highlighted by this research are useful for neighborhood associations, technology developers, and community organizers. They would also be useful to urban planners who are attempting to engage neighborhood residents via social media applications and platforms, or when they are analyzing results from community informatics projects that use social media. boyd (2011: 55) notes, "[t]he rise of social network sites has introduced ever-increasing populations to the trials and tribulations of navigating networked publics." In this instance, a neighborhood association gave social networking sites a try and was disappointed in the results. Their experience affirmed findings from previous research, such as, the need for pre-existing ties and issues with accessibility. However, other factors were uncovered which made neighbors hesitant to use social media (even those comfortable with social network sites) including: inequality of access and fears that some neighborhood residents might be left out (not democratic enough), concerns that social media would become the only communication outlet, expectations of residents that neighborhood communication should be face to face, and perceptions of social media as being too intimate and, simultaneously, too impersonal for the neighborhood context. These findings offer insight into the relationships between social media use and neighborhood contexts, give guidance to neighborhood associations on how to effectively adapt to new forms of communication, and suggest directions for further investigation into the potential and problems of social media for neighborhood use.

Bibliography

M. Ames, J. Go, J. Kaye, and M. Spasojevic, "Understanding Technology Choices and Values through Social Class," Proceedings of CSCW 2011, ACM Conference on Computer-Supported Cooperative Work (ACM Press, March 2011).

M. Arnold, "Intranets, Community, and Social Capital: The Case of William Bay," *Bulletin of Science Technology and Society* 23: 2 (2003) 78–87.

M. Arnold, M. Gibbs, and P. Wright, "Intranets and Local Community: 'Yes, an Intranet is all Very Well, but Do We Still Get Free Beer and a Barbeque?," in M. Huysman, E. Wenger, and V. Wulf, eds., *Communities and Technologies* (The Netherlands: Kluwer, B.V. Deventer, 2003) 185–204.

J.M. Berry, K.E. Portney, and K. Thomson, *The Rebirth of Urban Democracy* (Washington, DC: The Brookings Institution, 1993).

d. boyd, "Social Networking Sites as Networked Publics: Affordances, Dynamics, and Implications," in Z. Papacharissi, ed., *A Networked Self: Identity, Community, and Culture on Social Network Sites* (New York: Routledge, 2011) 39–58.

T.H. Carr, M.C. Dixon, and R.M. Ogles, "Perceptions of Community Life which Distinguish between Participants and Nonparticipants in a Neighborhood Self-Help Organization," *American Journal of Community Psychology* 4: 4 (1976) 357–366.

J. Carroll, *The Neighborhood in the Internet: Design Research Projects in Community Informatics* (New York: Routledge, 2012).

R.J. Chaskin, "Perspectives on Neighborhood and Community: A Review of the Literature," *Social Service Review* 71: 4 (1997) 521–547.

D.M. Chavis and A. Wandersman, "Sense of Community in the Urban Environment: A Catalyst for Participation and Community Development," *American Journal of Community Psychology* 18: 1 (1990) 55–81.

D. Cooperrider and M. Avita, eds., *Constructive Discourse and Human Organization: Advances in Appreciative Inquiry* (Bingley, UK: Emerald Group Publishing, 2004).

C.J. Coulton, M.Z. Jennings, & T. Chane, "How Big is My Neighborhood? Individual and Contextual Effects on Perceptions of Neighborhood Scale," *American Journal of Community Psychology* 51: 1–2 (2012) 40–50.

J. Cresswell, *Qualitative Inquiry and Research Design: Choosing Among Five Approaches* (Thousand Oaks, CA: Sage Publications, 2007).

B. Crump, "The Portability of Urban Ties," paper presented at Annual Meetings of the American Sociological Association, (Chicago, September, 1977)

W.K.D. Davies and I.J. Townshend, "How Do Community Associations Vary: The Structure of Community Associations in Calgary, Alberta," *Urban Studies* 31: 10 (1994) 1739–1761.

D.A. Dillman, *Mail and Internet Surveys: Second Edition* (New York: John Wiley & Sons, Inc., 2000).

A. Duany, E. Plater-Zyberk, and J. Speck, *Suburban Nation: The Rise of Sprawl and the Decline of the American Dream* (New York: North Point Press, 2000).

N. Ellison and d. boyd, "Sociality through Social Network Sites," in W. H. Dutton, ed., *The Oxford Handbook of Internet Studies* (Oxford: Oxford University Press, 2013) 151–172.

N. Ellison, C. Steinfield, and C. Lampe, "Spatially Bounded Online Social Networks and Social Capital: The Role of Facebook,"paper presented at the annual meeting of the *International Communication Association* (Dresden, June 2006).

N. Ellison, C. Steinfield, C. Lampe, "The Benefits of Facebook 'Friends': Social Capital and College Students' Use of Online Social Network Sites," *Journal of Computer-Mediated Communication* 12: 4 (2007) 1143–1168.

J. Evans-Cowley, "Planning in the Age of Facebook: the Role of Social Networking in Planning Processes," *GeoJournal* 75 (2010) 407–420.

J. Evans-Cowley and J. Hollander, "The New Generation of Public Participation: Internet-based Participation Tools," *Planning, Practice & Research* 25: 3 (2010) 397–408.

R.J. Firmino, "Planning the Unplannable: How Local Authorities Integrate Urban and ICT Policy Making," *Journal of Urban Technology* 12: 2 (2005) 49–69.

C. Fischer, *To Dwell Among Friends* (Chicago, IL: University of Chicago Press, 1982).

M. Foth, "Analyzing the Factors Influencing the Successful Design and Uptake of Interactive Systems to Support Social Networks in Urban Neighborhoods," *International Journal of Technology and Human Interaction* 2: 2 (2006a) 65–82.

M. Foth, "Facilitating Social Networking in Inner-City Neighborhoods," *IEEE Computer* 39: 9 (2006b) 44–50.

M. Gaved and M. Foth, "More than Wires, Pipes and Ducts: Some Lessons from Grassroots Networked Communities and Master-Planned Neighbourhoods," in R. Meersman, Z. Tari, and P. Herrero, eds., *Proceedings OTM (OnTheMove) Workshops* 2006.

T.J. Glynn, "Psychological Sense of Community: Measurement and Application," *Human Relations* 34: 7 (1981) 789–818.

A.M. Guest, J.K. Cover, R.L. Matsueda, and C.E. Kubrin, "Neighborhood Context and Neighboring Ties," *City & Community* 5: 4 (2006) 363–385.

M. Gurstein, "Welcome to the Journal of Community Informatics," *The Journal of Community Informatics* 1: 1 (2004) 2–4.

S.H. Haeberle, "Good Neighbors and Good Neighborhoods: Comparing Demographic and Environmental Influences on Neighborhood Activism," *State & Local Government Review* 18: 3 (1986) 109–116.

K. Hampton, "Grieving for a Lost Network: Collective Action in a Wired Suburb Special Issue: ICTs and Community Networking," *The Information Society* 19: 5 (2003) 417–428.

K. Hampton, "Neighborhoods in the Network Society: The e-Neighbors Study," *Information, Communication, and Society* 10: 5 (2007) 714–748.

K.N. Hampton and B. Wellman, "Netville Online and Offline: Observing and Surveying a Wired Suburb," *American Behavioral Scientist* 43: 3 (1999) 475–492.

K. Hampton and B. Wellman, "Grieving For A Lost Network: Collective Action Online in a Wired Suburb Special Issue: ICTs and Community Networking," *The Information Society* 19: 5 (2003a) 417–428.

K. Hampton and B. Wellman, "Neighboring in Netville: How the Internet Supports Community and Social Capital in a Wired Suburb," *City & Community* 2: 4 (2003b) 277–311.

K. Hampton, L.S. Goulet, L. Rainie, and K. Purcell, *Social Networking Sites and Our Lives* (Washington, DC: Pew Internet and American Life, 2011a).

K. Hampton, C. Lee, and E. Her, "How New Media Affords Network Diversity: Direct and Mediated Access to Social Capital Through Participation in Local Social Settings," *New Media & Society* 13: 7 (2011b) 1031–1049.

J. Hartley, *Uses of Television* (New York: Routledge, 1999).

J. Hillier, "Presumptive Planning: From Urban Design to Community Creation in One Move," in A.T. Fisher and C.C. Sonn, eds., *Psychological Sense of Community* (New York: Kluwer Academic/Plenum Publishers, 2002) 43–67.

J. Hollan and S. Stornetta, "Beyond Being There," *CHI '92 Proceedings of the SIGCHI Conference on Human Factors in Computing Systems* (1992) 119–125.

Indian Hills Neighborhood Association, *Indian Hills Neighborhood Association (Brochure)* (Lawrence, KS: Indian Hills Neighborhood Association, 2003).

B. Johnson and G. Halegoua, "Can Social Media Save a Neighborhood Organization?," paper presented at Using ICT, Social Media, and Mobile Technologies to Foster Self-Organization in Urban and Neighborhood Governance (Delft, The Netherlands, May 2013).

A. Kavanaugh and M. Patterson, "The Impact of Community Computer Networks on Social Capital and Community Involvement in Blacksburg," in B. Wellman and C. Haythornthwaite, eds., *The Internet in Everyday Life* (Malden, MA: Blackwell, 2002) 325–344.

A.L. Kavanaugh, T.T. Zin, M.B. Rosson, J.M. Carroll, J. Schmitz, and B.J. Kim, "Local Groups Online: Political Learning and Participation," *Computer Supported Cooperative Work* 16: 4–5 (2007) 375–395.

J.B. Kim, A.L. Kavanaugh, and K. Hult, "Local Community Groups and Internet Use," *International Journal of Technology, Knowledge and Society* 2: 7 (2007) 207–221.

M. Koschmann and N.M. Laster, "Communicative Tensions of Community Organizing: The Case of a Local Neighborhood Association," *Western Journal of Communication* 75: 1 (2011) 28–51.

M. Kotler, *Neighborhood Government: The Local Foundations of Political Life* (Indianapolis: The Bobbs-Merril Co, 1969).

B. Looker, "Microcosms of Democracy: Imagining the City Neighborhood in World War II-Era America," *Journal of Social History* 44: 2 (2010) 351–378.

S. Lopes, "Building Community Power Structures, 1984-1998," in D. Domer and B. Watkins, eds., *Embattled Lawrence: Conflict & Community* (Lawrence, KS: University of Kansas Continuing Education, 2001) 277–288.

L. Mandarano, M. Meenar, and C. Steins, "Building Social Capital in the Digital Age of Civic Engagement," *Journal of Planning Literature* 25 (2010) 123–135.

M.L. Martinez, M. Black, and R.H. Starr, "Factorial Structure of the Perceived Neighborhood Scale (PNS): A Test of Longitudinal Invariance," *Journal of Community Psychology* 30: 1 (2002) 23–43.

B.A. McClenahan, *The Changing Urban Neighborhood, from Neighbor to Nigh-Dweller* (Los Angeles, CA: University of Southern California Studies, 1929).

R.D. McKenzie, "The Neighborhood: A Study of Local Life in the City of Columbus, Ohio—Concluded," *American Journal of Sociology* 27: 6 (1922) 780–799.

D. Meredith, S. Ewing, and J. Thomas, "Neighbourhood Renewal and Government by Community: The Atherton Gardens Network," *International Journal of Cultural Policy* 10: 1 (2004) 85–101.

D.J. Monti Jr., C. Butler, A. Curley, K. Tilney, and M.F. Weiner, "Private Lives and Public Worlds: Changes in Americans' Social Ties and Civic Attachments in the Late-20th Century," *City & Community* 2: 2 (2003) 143–163.

D.A. Norman, *The Psychology of Everyday Things* (New York: Basic Books, 1988).

D.A. Norman, "Affordance, Convention, and Design," *Interactions* 6: 3 (1999) 38–43.

P. Olson, "Urban Neighborhood Research: Its Development and Current Focus," *Urban Affairs Review* 17: 4 (1982) 491–518.

S.R. Oropesa, "The Ironies of Human Resource Mobilization by Neighborhood Associations," *Nonprofit and Voluntary Sector Quarterly* 24: 3 (1995) 235–252.

A. Pattavina, G. Pierce, and A. Saiz, "Urban Neighborhood Information Systems: Crime Prevention and Control Applications," *Journal of Urban Technology* 9: 1 (2002) 37–56.

D.D. Perkins and A.D. Long, "Neighborhood Sense of Community and Social Capital: A Multi-Level Analysis," in A.T. Fisher, C.C. Sonn, and B.J. Bishop, eds., *Psychological Sense of Community: Research, Applications, and Implications* (New York: Kluwer Academic/ Plenum Publishers, 2002) 291–318.

K. Pigg and L. Crank, "Building Community Social Capital: The Potential and Promise of Information and Communications Technologies," *The Journal of Community Informatics* 1: 1 (2004) 58–73.

N. Pineda, "Facebook Tips: What's the Difference between a Facebook Page and Group?" February 24, 2010. https://www.facebook.com/notes/324706977130

R. Pinkett, "Community Technology and Community Building: Early Results from the Creating Community Connections Project Special Issue: ICTs and Community Networking," *The Information Society: An International Journal* 19: 5 (2003) 365–379.

R.D. Putnam, *Bowling Alone: The Collapse and Revival of American Community* (New York: Simon & Schuster, 2000).

L. Rainie, K. Purcell, and A. Smith, *The Social Side of the Internet* (Washington, DC: Pew Internet and American Life Project, January 18, 2011).

L.G. Rivlin, "The Neighborhood, Personal Identity, and Group Affiliation," in I. Altman and A. Wandersman, eds., *Neighborhood and Community Environments* (New York: Plenum, 1987) 1–34.

Saguaro Seminar, *2000 Social Capital Benchmark Survey*. http://www.ropercenter.uconn.edu/scc_bench.html Accessed August, 2005.

D. Schuler, *New Community Networks: Wired for Change* (New York: Addison-Wesley Publishing Company, 1996).

D.V. Shah, N. Kwak, and R.L. Holbert, "'Connecting' and 'Disconnecting' With Civic Life: Patterns of Internet Use and the Production of Social Capital," *Political Communication* 18 (2001) 141–162.

S.T. Sigmon, S.R. Whitcomb, and C.R. Snyder, "Psychological Home," in A.T. Fisher, C.C. Sonn, and B.J. Bishop, eds., *Psychological Sense of Community* (New York: Kluwer Academic/Plenum Publishers, 2002) 25–42.

C. Silver, "Neighborhood Planning in Historical Perspective," *Journal of the American Planning Association* 51: 2 (1985) 161–174.

A. Smith, *Neighbors Online* (Washington DC: Pew Internet and American Life Project, June 9, 2010).

P.W. Speer, J. Hughey, L.K. Gensheimer, and W. Adams-Leavitt, "Organizing for Power: A Comparative Case Study," *Journal of Community Psychology* 23 (1995) 57–73.

A. Strauss and J. Corbin, *Basics of Qualitative Research: Grounded Theory Procedures and Techniques* (Newbury Park, CA: Sage Publications, 1990).

A. Strauss and J. Corbin, *Basics of Qualitative Research: Techniques and Procedures for Developing Grounded Theory* (Thousand Oaks, CA: Sage Publications, 1998).

Y. Takhteyev, A. Gruzd, and B. Wellman, "Geography of Twitter networks," *Social Networks* 34: 1 (2012) 73–81.

D.G. Unger and A. Wandersman, "The Importance of Neighbors: The Social, Cognitive, and Affective Components of Neighboring," *American Journal of Community Psychology* 13: 2 (1985) 139–169.

United States Bureau of the Census, *State and County QuickFacts* (Washington, D.C. United States Bureau of the Census, 2013) http://quickfacts.census.gov/qfd/states/20/2038900.html Accessed April 25, 2013.

A. Wandersman, P. Florin, R. Friedman, and R. Meier, "Who Participates, Who Does Not, and Why? An Analysis of Voluntary Neighborhood Organizations in the United States and Israel," *Sociological Forum* 2: 3 (1987) 534–555.

D.I. Warren, "The Functional Diversity of Urban Neighborhoods," *Urban Affairs Review* 13: 2 (1977) 151–180.

B. Wellman, "From Little Boxes to Loosely Bounded Networks: The Privatization and Domestication of Community," in J. Abu-Lughod, ed., *Sociology for the Twenty-First Century: Continuities and Cutting Edges* (Chicago: University of Chicago Press, 1999) 94–114.

B. Wellman and K. Hampton, "Living Networked On and Off Line," *Contemporary Sociology* 28: 6 (1999) 648–654.

B. Wellman and K. Hampton, "Neighboring in Netville. How the Internet Supports Community and Social Capital in a Wired Suburb," City & Community 2: 4 (2003) 277–311.

B. Wellman, P. Carrington, and A. Hall, "Networks as Personal Communities," in Barry Wellman and S.D. Berkowitz, eds., *Social Structures: A Network Analysis* (Cambridge: Cambridge University Press, 1988) 130–184.

B. Wellman, A. Haase, J. Witte, and K. Hampton, "Does the Internet Increase, Decrease, or Supplement Social Capital? Social Networks, Participation and Community Commitment," *American Behavioral Scientist* 45: 3 (2001) 436–455.

S. Yardi and d. boyd, "Tweeting from the Town Square: Measuring Geographic Local Networks," *Proceedings of the Fourth International AAAI Conference on Weblogs and Social Media* (2010).

The Digital Divide in Citizen-Initiated Government Contacts: A GIS Approach

Sara Cavallo, Joann Lynch, and Peter Scull

ABSTRACT *As the role of information and communications technologies (ICTs) grows, governments have seen the Geoweb and Web 2.0 as an opportunity to increase citizen involvement through e-government which provides citizens with the ability to record and share information. 311 services represent citizens' most direct contact with local governments in the form of volunteered geographic information (VGI) empowering citizens with the means of solving community issues. Past studies have examined VGI and e-government use finding patterns of a digital divide with survey data; yet, further research which allows for the visualization of these patterns using citizen-generated data is needed to understand the link between users and the content they create. This paper seeks to explore the relationship between sociodemographic status and 311 service request frequency in three cities within the United States using geographic information systems (GIS) and regression analysis. Results suggest the potential existence of a digital divide and that the demographic profile of a city plays a role in participation in e-government.*

Introduction

> E-Government Act of 2002:
> To promote use of the Internet and other information technologies to provide increased opportunities for citizen participation in Government ....To promote the use of the Internet and emerging technologies within and across Government agencies to provide citizen-centric Government information and services.... To promote better informed decision making by policy makers. (E-Government Act of 2002)

With the rise of Web 2.0, users no longer passively receive information, but instead partake in content creation (Johnson and Sieber, 2013). The geographic component of Web 2.0, the geospatial web (GeoWeb), consists of geographic applications and services which involve the collection and sharing of locational data (Cinnamon and Schuurman, 2012). Goodchild (2007) defines the participation of citizens in the creation of geographic information as volunteered geographic information

(VGI), a derivative of Web 2.0 user-generated content. Geographic data is now a blend of information from citizens, private firms, and governments (Elwood, 2010). Turner (2006) identifies web users who employ geospatial technologies without geographic expertise as neogeographers. Today, the GeoWeb's user-friendly websites and phone applications provide the platforms necessary to create and share VGI. In turn, neogeographers now have a means of recording and creating locational data to support social interaction, political empowerment, and community security.

Governments have seen the Geoweb and Web 2.0 as an opportunity to build upon existing citizen-to-government-to-citizen (C2G2C) communication channels (Johnson and Sieber, 2013). Initially, "e-government" services merely meant access to documents and government services online (Dugdale et al., 2005). However, the development of ICTs has allowed government agencies to expand e-government and use the Internet as a means of two-way interaction with citizens where transactions can occur; requests can be filed and fulfilled through ICT tools (Dugdale et al., 2005). Today, these transaction services, defined as "e-government," serve as a platform for citizen feedback and a means of government accountability (Dugdale et al., 2005; Hall and Owens, 2011). Services such as the 311 system, a citizen request hotline, have been integrated into government websites in the United States to streamline citizens' transactions with local, state, and federal governments (NCR, 2009). Designed with the aim of increasing citizens' access and communication, 311 services are perceived as a means of citizen empowerment that provide the government with feedback in the form of VGI (Elwood et al., 2012). For example, when citizens submit a request via the 311 platform, the location of the issue and the submission date are recorded, thereby, providing citizens with a timeline for the fulfillment of all requests submitted. Some cities with the most comprehensive 311 services now offer smartphone applications that allow citizens to tag their geographic location within a service request (for example, NYC311, 2014; SF311, 2014).

While proponents of e-government emphasize the benefits of innovation, critics argue that the digital divide, a technology access and skills divide within the population, will increase inequalities (Bélanger and Carter, 2009). Thus, the rapid adoption of new forms of e-government, like that of 311 which is based on volunteered geographic information, warrants further analysis to evaluate how the submission of public service requests are distributed throughout the city.

This paper seeks to evaluate citizen participation in these new forms of e-government through empirical research on 311 service requests in three cities: New York City, San Francisco, and Washington DC. This work contributes to our understanding of e-government and the digital divide through answering two questions: How do different areas within these cities contribute to 311 service requests? What are the implications for cities that face differential intra-urban participation in submitting municipal service requests? This study uses a novel approach to evaluate service request participation through combining volunteered geographic records of submitted service requests with socio-demographic data using GIS and statistical modeling.

The paper will be organized as follows: The first section provides a brief overview of the changing forms of e-government and the implications of those changes for citizen and government interaction. The second section provides a description of 311 services. Issues of the digital divide and participation in 311 are discussed in the third section. The next section offers statistics that detail the socio-demographic characteristics of the areas using the 311 services. Also offered in this section are the statistical methods used in the analysis. The final sections present results and discussion of the implications along with suggestions for further research.

The New e-Government

Public access to information and communications technologies (ICTs) is increasing as services move online. As a result, there has been a push to integrate new technologies into government services in order to increase efficiency and improve the dissemination of information to the public (Asgarkhani, 2007; Dugdale et al., 2005). Often, firms within the private sector quickly adopt new technologies to remain competitive, while the public sector is slower to conform (Asgarkhani, 2007). In part, the public sector's innovation lag is due to caution in government initiatives as the effects on public policy are more far-reaching than those of private firms (Wolhers, 2009). In addition, the public sector often lacks the ability to quickly acquire technology and experienced personnel due to financial constraints (Evans-Cowley and Conroy, 2006; Wolhers, 2009). Thus, government institutions must weigh the costs against the potential benefits when deciding whether or not to implement e-government services (Evans-Conroy and Cowley, 2006). Today, most national, state, and local government institutions in the United States have a form of e-government, but the complexity of services varies by resource availability (Wolhers, 2009).

The most basic form of e-government is government-to-citizen (G2C) communication, a one-way communication channel that provides access to information regarding government services and processes such as contacts for local representatives (Asgarkhani, 2007). G2C interaction allows for greater transparency in the public sector, and the government now risks increased public scrutiny. This shift towards greater accountability requires that governments quickly respond to citizens' needs and ensure that all groups are equally included (Dugdale et al., 2005; Wolhers, 2009). The second wave of e-government involves citizen participation through feedback, or citizen-to-government (C2G) communication (Asgarkhani, 2007; Johnson and Sieber, 2013). C2G communication via e-government portals provides citizens a platform to increase their participation in government online which fosters what is termed "e-democracy" (Wolhers, 2009).

The advent of Web 2.0 initiated a third wave of e-government that provides citizens with an opportunity to participate in the generation of online content surrounding public matters. Today, citizens can initiate the process of data creation, cataloguing, and reporting issues within the community as well as organizing online forums for subjects surrounding government policies, initiatives, and services (Dugdale et al., 2005; Johnson and Sieber, 2012). As producers of information, citizens can use new e-government services to become more involved in local political processes and to increase communication within the community and between the community and the government, creating more inclusive channels of communication (Johnson and Sieber, 2012; Maguire and Longley 2005; Wolhers, 2009). With more information, the government can now respond more effectively to citizens' needs.

The new e-government supports citizen-to-government-to-citizen (C2G2C) communication rather than solely G2C or C2G communication. C2G2C creates a dialog centered on citizen's concerns (Johnson and Sieber, 2013). In this way, the use of new e-government services has been described as a marketing strategy for governments to directly engage with citizens by increasing transparency and reducing citizens' cynicism towards public services (Berman, 1997; Elbahnasawy, 2014; Johnson and Sieber, 2012).

311 and Citizen Involvement

The 311 service was created by the Federal Communications Commission in 1997 as a part of the larger shift in government services towards more citizen-driven approaches (Thomas, 2005). Baltimore was the first city to adopt the service, and, today, over 20 cities in the United States have adopted similar services with many more in development (Schwester et al., 2009; OPEN311.org).

311 is a citizen request hotline through which citizens can call in or report municipal issues via phone or any Internet-enabled device. These municipal issues range from sanitation and waste management, noise complaints and vermin sightings, to infrastructure repairs and damage reports. In this way, 311 serves as the non-emergency alternative to 911.

Before 311, citizens found it challenging to obtain information and support due to local bureaucracy. Often, citizen contacts that were not received by the appropriate agency burdened municipal offices that served other functions (Thomas, 2005). Most prominently, the strain on the 911 service of non-emergency calls created a lag in the system that had the potential to preclude other, urgent emergencies (Schwester et al., 2009). Citizens also reached out to public officials when there was no clear contact system for voicing complaints, placing further stress on the local government infrastructure (NCR, 2009). Without a central agency, there was little government accountability, culminating an overwhelming sense of distrust in the government and lack of motivation to participate in government initiatives (Thomas, 2005). Without the proper feedback mechanisms, governments could not work towards fulfilling citizen needs (Thomas, 2005).

311 services work to solve these problems by providing a central agency through which to channel service and information requests without disrupting other government agencies (Thomas, 2005). Further, it is suggested that these services foster trust between the government and the public, increasing transparency (NCR, 2009).

Unlike earlier telephone-based 311 systems, modern 311 services represent citizens' most direct contact with local governments in the form of VGI. Through this system, residents are able to report any problems, complaints, or praise for local policies and services via an online portal or on a mobile device. By providing a way to monitor government accountability these services are purported to create an instant connection with municipal institutions providing citizens with the appropriate means of solving community issues. Citizens can now view the progress made on their requests online and see that requests are being handled quickly and efficiently (Schwester et al., 2009). Further, through interactive platforms such as maps and online websites, citizens are also able to explore service requests and activity posted by others to explore current issues within their community or the city more broadly.

The Digital Divide

The E-government Act of 2002 was created to increase access to government services and citizen participation in government, but for these standards to be met, citizens must have equal access to services (Baird et al., 2012). The digital divide represents the gap between those who have access to the Internet and the knowledge to navigate it and those who do not (Bélanger and Carter, 2009). Therefore, governments must be cautious if certain groups within the community have unequal or limited access to these services. Past studies have used surveys to examine VGI and e-government use finding patterns of a digital divide, but the degree to which the digital divide affects certain groups has not been affirmed (Bélanger and Carter, 2009; Elwood et al., 2012; Hall and Owens, 2011).

However, in this paper, we reference a digital divide not in the sense of *access* to Internet services like 311 (although that may play a role), but rather in terms of how participation varies in space. Regardless of the motivation behind who contributes, 311 has become the central authority behind municipal city service provision, and it has moved almost exclusively into the digital realm. Thus, if certain areas are not reporting as much as others, it suggests many alternatives: Perhaps these areas are unaware of the service, or do not use certain types of infrastructure, or maybe they are involved in many other activities and do not have time to notice or document these issues. This paper does not seek to answer the question of *why* citizens choose to contribute or not but rather the question of *where* and what are the characteristics of places which do not contribute. We see this issue as similar to that of voter turnout. Individuals with a variety of motivations or limiting factors (from apathy to limited access) do not vote. Despite the clear difference (some are not able to vote versus some choose not to), both groups are opted out of the democratic process. Here, individuals are opted out of municipal services.

Being opted out of municipal services is different from voter turnout in that it creates a material reality for the residents of that area—lack of participation signals lack of service provision and has implications for the physical infrastructure (Gilbert et al., 2008). Further, the areas which have fewer service requests are missing out on the benefits of the C2G2C interaction and the ability to participate in the "conversation" around municipal services.

The growing social media identity of 311, as the use of mobile applications has continued to rise, has implications as well for the areas which have different levels of participation in submitting 311 service requests. Areas with high concentrations of requests have the added benefit of social capital. More users contributing service requests may foster a greater community in certain areas, perhaps focused around certain issues (such as potholes). Hampton and Wellman (2003) found that an online neighborhood forum led to greater community involvement of the residents and more public participation. The sense of community created by the ability to interact with others and the municipal government through online maps and mobile applications has the ability to work in similar ways. Areas which do not contribute as much to 311 service requests miss out on this opportunity to create social capital within the neighborhood context.

Methods

Study Sites

The 311 systems in New York, San Francisco, and Washington DC serve approximately 9.5 million people (US Census Bureau 2010a, 2010b, 2010c). As economic hubs and sources of influence in their respective regions, these cities provide geographically and culturally diverse case studies. Identifying if a digital divide might exist within these populations can inform future policies and government initiatives which may be used as models for other municipalities. To evaluate the effectiveness of a citizen-engagement system, it is necessary to identify the characteristics of those areas that submit 311 service requests.

New York City began offering 311 services in 2003 in order to consolidate information for citizens and provide an outlet for citizens to voice their concerns (Schwester et al., 2009). Through an online site, residents are able to monitor their requests and see the expected repair time. The 311 Program in San Francisco began in 2005, and the city adopted online services in addition to traditional phone-based methods in 2008 (CCSF, 2012). Since then, the online presence of 311 has grown and the municipal government is now making strides toward using social media such as Twitter, in their data collection process. Through the DC 311 service, those within the Washington DC area are able to call 3-1-1 or visit the city's website dedicated to 311 to submit a request for information or a complaint (DC, 2012). All three cities have an online portal which allows those who have registered a request to log on and check the status of their request. These data do not include the type of technology used to submit the request, but there is a feature that allows visitors to map the opened, closed, and pending requests by a variety of variables.

Service Request Data

Data on 311 service requests are collected via the municipal websites of the three cities. The data is publicly available for download in a variety of formats under the Freedom of Information Act. New York City, San Francisco, and Washington DC organize their 311 services under the Open311, open source data platform. Open 311 facilitates the adoption of government services like 311 around the United States by providing web-infrastructure that is easily customized and integrated into municipal governments (Open311.org).

Each city produces over a million 311 service requests per year, and these requests are organized using a service request classification system unique to each city. In order to standardize comparison across and within cities, the analysis is limited to service requests in 2011 that are classified as parking meter repair, sidewalk and street repair, potholes, and traffic signal repair. Requests pertaining to repairs of city-owned infrastructure, such as roads and sidewalks that are evenly distributed throughout the cities, are chosen to limit the effects of biases tied to the socioeconomic status of residents. Other characteristics, such as residential repairs and consumer complaints, by definition, are tied to socio-demographic status. For example, low-income households are more likely to reside in low quality housing, and thus, require more housing repairs. Therefore, variables of this nature are excluded from the study.

Further, these three categories of service requests have important implications for city residents. Traffic light repair, sidewalk maintenance, street repair, and parking meter repair have substantial costs when left unaddressed. In terms of personal safety, sidewalk damage and potholes pose the risk of accidents and high healthcare costs along with car repair costs. Traffic light repair has important implications for traffic accidents which also incur high health and financial costs. Finally, parking meter problems may result in costs associated with parking violation fees and towing charges.

Socio-demographic Data

Citizens' identities influence their online behavior (Crutcher and Zook, 2009). Thus, a citizen's choice to generate VGI is influenced by their demographic characteristics. Previous studies show that despite increasing availability of the Internet, factors such as gender, race, ethnicity, education, age, income, citizenship status, housing tenure, and parental status still influence participation in online activities (Crutcher and Zook, 2009; Stephens, 2013). Therefore, these variables are included in the analysis. Data on these topics are gathered from two main sources within the US Census Bureau: the 2010 Census Demographic Profile (CDP) and the American Community Survey 5-Year Estimates (ACS). A summary of the variables and their expected relationships on 311 service requests are included in Table 1.

Income. Government use of information and communication technologies (ICTs) as a means of citizen outreach can exclude members of the population who do not have the skills and resources necessary to participate. Van Aerschot and

Table 1: Data sources and predictions.

Variable	Source	Prediction
311 Requests	NYC311, DC311, SF311	n/a
Income		
Mean Income	ACS	+
General Housing and Population Characteristics		
Median Age	CDP	−
% Female	CDP	−
% African American	CDP	−
% Asian	CDP	−
% Latino	CDP	−
% Households with Children	CDP	+
% Occupied Housing Units	CDP	+
% Rented Units	CDP	−
Education and Citizenship		
% High School	ACS	+
% Foreign Born	ACS	−
% Naturalized	ACS	−
% Non-Citizen	ACS	−

Note: CDP = Census Demographic Profile
ACS = American Community Survey
(-) Less likely to make 311 service requests
(+) More likely to make 311 service requests
Source: US Census Bureau 2010a, 2010b, 2010c, 2011a, 2011b, 2011c, NYC 311, DC 311, SF 311.

Rodousakis (2008) identify low-income groups as more than two times less likely to use the Internet in comparison to high-income groups suggesting that low-income groups are less likely to have both the ability to access ICT resources and the skills necessary to use these technologies. With an increase in e-government initiatives, this problem may become more pronounced.

General Population and Housing Characteristics. Traditionally, disenfranchized demographic groups are associated with less access to the Internet and participation in local government. Stephens (2013) suggests that biases found within society are revealed in the demographics of those who contribute VGI. In particular, men are the dominant producers of data on the Geoweb (Stephens, 2013). Further, minority populations have been historically underrepresented in both citizen-initiated contacts and Internet access (Crutcher and Zook, 2009). Similarly, with the emergence of new technologies, older populations may not have the skills or the information necessary to participate in Internet-based services (Van Aerschot and Rodousakis, 2008). The elderly may face significant disadvantages in using e-government compared to younger residents who are more likely to have a better understanding of newer ICTs as a result of increased exposure and education (Van Aerschot and Rodousakis, 2008).

Homeowners and households with children are likely to have more investment within the community and may raise the likelihood of participation in citizen-initiated services according to Thomas and Streib (2003). Owners of housing units may be more apt to report a problem in their neighborhood because they value the upkeep of their home environment in the long run, in contrast with renters, who have only temporary housing tenure; similarly, the long-term maintenance of the municipal area has implications for parents as they want to ensure that their children are raised in a safe environment (Thomas and Streib, 2003).

Education and Citizenship Status. Education is a necessary requirement for full participation in e-government services. Information literacy and computer training provide citizens with the ability to access these services. As suggested by Van Aerschot and Rodousakis (2008), with greater levels of education, citizens are more aware of the services provided by the government and as a result, are often more involved in the democratic process. In contrast, recent migrants may not be familiar with the US government structure or may face language barriers, both of which present challenges to participation in e-government services (Van Aerschot and Rodousakis, 2008).

Summary Statistics

311 service requests are imported into a GIS that includes the spatial information associated with the service request. In order to allow for comparison of census data and 311 request frequency, the service request data points are aggregated to the census tract level, creating a count of service requests per tract. Figure 1 illustrates the total count of those service requests that were selected for analysis (parking meter repair, sidewalk and street repair, potholes, and traffic signal repair). The census tracts for each individual city are divided into five quantile classes using a bi-color symbology scheme; the median service

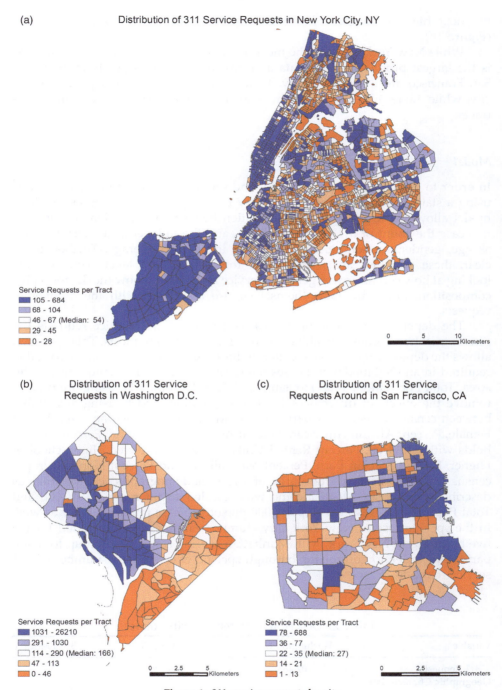

Figure 1: 311 service requests by city.
Source: US Census Bureau 2010a, 2010b, 2010c, 2011a, 2011b, 2011c.

request value is symbolized in white, while those census tracts both above and below are symbolized in blue and red respectively. The City of San Francisco (Figure 1c) has the fewest number of requests; New York City (Figure 1a) has the next highest number of service requests, followed by Washington DC (Figure 1b).

While New York City has the most tracts of the three cities, Washington DC is the largest producer of 311 data and has more requests per tract than both San Francisco and New York City. Table 2 presents the summary statistics by city, while Table 3 breaks down the statistics to the average across all census tracts.

Model

In order to evaluate how demography and service requests interact, we will be using a statistical model termed Ordinary Least Squares [OLS] regression. This model allows us to measure the association between a dependent variable, in this case the count of 311 service requests, and the independent variables such as age, gender, race-ethnic structure, and income on average. Further, to be clear, these variables are measured at the census tract level. Thus we are looking at how certain spaces generate service requests and how the demographic composition, not individuals themselves, are associated with the number of requests.

The dependent variable of interest is a count of 311 service requests per census tract transformed by taking the log of the count of requests. This operation allows the dependent variable to better fit the assumption of a normal distribution required in an OLS model and eases interpretation of results. Land Area, Water Area, Total Population, Total Housing, and Total Occupied Housing are used to remove the effects of differences in area, population, and housing availability between census tracts on 311 participation. Mean Income, Median Age, Percent Female, Percent African American, Percent Asian, Percent Latino, Percent Households with Children, Percent Rented Units, Percent Completed High School or Higher, Percent Foreign Born, Percent Naturalized, and Percent Non-citizen per census tract are used as measures of the sociodemographic composition as described previously. Mean income was rescaled to intervals of $10,000 and Total Population is rescaled to per 1,000 persons to ease interpretability as well. In the specific case of New York City, dummy variables were included for the five boroughs of New York, with Manhattan serving as the base group for comparison in order to control for borough-specific effects on the number of 311 service requests.

Table 2: Descriptive statistics—city totals.

Variable	Washington DC	New York City	San Francisco
311 Requests	207,465	155,690	9,990
Geographic Characteristics			
Land Area (sq km)	158.1	783.8	121.4
Water Area (sq km)	18.9	429.5	479.2
General Housing and Population Characteristics			
Population	601,723	8,175,133	805,235
Housing Units	296,719	3,371,062	345,811
Census Tracts	179	2,167	197

Source: US Census Bureau 2010a, 2010b, 2010c, 2011a, 2011b, 2011c, NYC 311, DC 311, SF 311.

Table 3: Descriptive statistics—average per census tract.

Variable	Washington DC	New York City	San Francisco
311 Requests	1,159	71.8	50.7
Geographic Characteristics			
Land Area (sq m)	883,322.2	361,717.7	616,243.5
Water Area (sq m)	105,502.6	198,213	2,432,438
Income			
Mean Income	83,967.6	70,427.6	98,995.1
General Housing and Population Characteristics			
Population	3,361.6	3,772.6	4,087.5
Median Age	35.4	35.7	38.8
% Female	52.7	51.6	48.5
% African American	57	28.5	7.6
% Asian	4	13.6	33.4
% Latino	8.2	26.3	14.6
% Households with Children	19.2	28.7	17.3
Housing Units	1,657.6	1,555.6	1,913.4
% Occupied Housing Units	89.8	96.9	91.2
% Rented Units	57.1	64.1	61.7
Education and Citizenship			
% High School	85	77.1	85.1
% Foreign Born	11.3	36.1	33.7
% Naturalized	39.6	52.9	59.6
% Non-Citizen	58.1	44.6	38.8
Census Tracts	179	2,167	197

Source: US Census Bureau 2010a, 2010b, 2010c, 2011a, 2011b, 2011c, NYC 311, DC 311, SF 311.

Results

The model is statistically significant for all three cities (See Table 4). The model for Washington DC performs best in terms of how much of the variance in the data is explained by our model. Washington DC is followed in performance by San Francisco and New York City. *The coefficients presented in Table 4 can be interpreted using the phrase: with a one unit increase/decrease in an independent variable (one of the sociodemographic characteristics), there is an associated 100*[value]% increase/decrease in 311 service requests on average.*

The San Francisco model accounts for 48 percent of the variance in 311 service request data. Racial composition (as measured by the percentage of African Americans), age, the percentage of families, education, and citizenship within the tract are all statistically significant. Race had a negative association with 311 service requests suggesting that for every one percentage point increase in race composition as measured by the percent of African Americans in a census tract, there was a 2.4 percent decrease in the number of requests on average. Median age has a positive relationship, meaning that older areas of the city are areas with a higher number of requests (about 3 percent) as well. Higher education rates and percentage of households with children are also associated with decreased 311 participation.

In Washington DC, race, ethnicity, age, parental status, and education explain 64 percent of the variance in the geography of 311 services requests. Race, as measured by percent Asian is the only variable with a positive relationship to the dependent variable, 311 requests, and it has one of the largest associations across all of the results for the three cities: A one percentage point increase in

Table 4: Regression coefficients.

	Log (311 Service Requests)		
	Washington D.C.	San Francisco	New York City
Land Area (sq m)	**0.1125**	**0.5194***	**0.3507***
	(0.16)	(0.12)	(0.03)
Water Area (sq m)	**0.298**	**-0.1968***	**-0.1569***
	(0.22)	(0.06)	(0.04)
Mean Income	**0.0767**	**-0.0237**	**0.0360***
	(0.05)	(0.03)	(0.01)
Population	**0.2439+**	**0.2264***	**0.1041***
	(0.13)	(0.04)	(0.01)
Median Age	**-0.0378+**	**0.0262+**	**-0.0117***
	(0.02)	(0.02)	(0.00)
% Female	**-0.0372+**	**0.0024**	**-0.0284***
	(0.02)	(0.01)	(0.00)
% African American	**-0.0041**	**-0.0244***	**-0.0040***
	(0.01)	(0.01)	(0.00)
% Asian	**0.1538***	**0.0074**	**0.0025+**
	(0.03)	(0.01)	(0.18)
% Latino	**-0.0368***	**0.0111**	**-0.0045***
	(0.02)	(0.01)	(0.00)
% Households with Children	**-0.0751***	**-0.0481***	**-0.0086***
	(0.01)	(0.01)	(0.00)
% Occupied Housing Units	**-0.0225**	**-0.0247**	**0.0014**
	(0.01)	(0.02)	(0.00)
% Rented Units	**-0.0092**	**0.0077**	**0.0017+**
	(0.01)	(0.01)	(0.00)
% High School	**-0.0407***	**-0.0241***	**0.0008**
	(0.01)	(0.01)	(0.00)
% Foreign Born	**-0.0002**	**-0.0193***	**-0.0018**
	(0.00)	(0.01)	(0.00)
% Naturalized	**0.0063**	**0.0009**	**0.0039***
	(0.00)	(0.01)	(0.00)
% Non-Citizen	**0.0052**	**0.0078**	**0.0050***
	(0.00)	(0.01)	(0.00)
Bronx			**-0.2617***
			(0.07)
Brooklyn			**-0.0801**
			(0.07)
Queens			**-0.1352+**
			(0.07)
Staten Island			**0.2437***
			(0.10)
Cons.	**13.98798***	**6.0125***	**4.9893***
	(2.38)	(2.67)	(0.32)
N	178	194	2135
R2R2	0.676	0.519	0.403
Adjusted R2Adjusted R2	0.644	0.476	0.397

Standard errors in parentheses $+ p < 0.10$, $*p < 0.05$.

the Asian population of a census tract is coupled with a 15 percent increase in service requests on average. The family composition variable also had a strong relationship with 311 requests in the opposite direction. With more families in a tract, there is a 7.5 percent decrease in the number of service requests on average. Both of these findings are in contrast to our initial predictions.

New York City's 311 service request distribution model explains 40 percent of the variance and is explained by gender, race, ethnicity, age, housing tenure, income, and citizenship status and households with children. In this case, mean income has a positive association with 311 requests: with an increase in mean income by $10,000, there is a 3 percent increase in service requests by census tract on average. Age, gender, and family structure have negative relationships with requests ranging from around a 1 to 3 percent decrease on average in the face of a one unit increase in these variables. At the same time, race-ethnic structure, housing tenure, and citizenship are significantly related to 311 requests, but the effects are relatively small. Renters, percent naturalized and percent noncitizen, and percent Asian are associated with positive, yet larger numbers of 311 requests, while percent African American and percent Latino are associated with fewer requests. Looking at the borough variables, all but Brooklyn are significant. Compared to Manhattan, census tracts within the Bronx and Queens are associated with fewer requests while Staten Island has more.

Discussion

The results suggest that the demographic profile of a city plays a pivotal role in who participates in and accesses the benefits of e-government. Crutcher and Zook (2009) conducted a study in post-Katrina New Orleans that identifies a highly racialized geography of volunteered information. These findings support our results that both an intra-urban digital divide exists and the nature of this divide is context specific. The contrast between cities highlights the importance of scale in understanding the digital divide. While previous studies on the national level show a digital divide across income, age, and education, these results may mask ethnic and racial inequalities specific to certain regions or cities (Bélanger and Carter, 2009). By focusing on intra-urban patterns, racial and ethnic disparities become more visible. Small-scale research on the digital divide can inform more effective locally directed policies which work to promote more inclusion in 311 services by increasing outreach and participation.

In New York City, the results indicate that areas with higher percentages of lower income households, older citizens, women, African Americans, Latinos, and households with children are associated with submitting fewer service requests, suggesting that these demographic groups are being opted out of participation in 311 services. Contrary to our initial hypotheses, areas with higher concentrations of renters, naturalized citizens, and noncitizens are associated with more service requests. These unique findings affirm the importance of context specific analysis, particularly in understanding the spatial aspects of municipal service distribution.

Results suggest that areas with higher percentages of women, Latino populations, households with children, and those with at least a high school education may face a digital divide in participation in 311 services in Washington DC. Tracts with higher percentages of Asian populations are associated with more service requests suggesting that this group may have greater access to the benefits of 311 services such as the opportunity for engaging with others in the community and generating neighborhood social capital. Educational attainment does not correspond to expectations and may be explained by the concentration of service requests in the city center as more affluent and highly educated citizens are concentrated in the north (Census, 2011).

In San Francisco, census tracts which contain higher percentages of households with children, African American households, foreign born, and those with at least a high school education are associated with fewer service requests. However, the number of service requests in San Francisco is concentrated in the downtown area (See Figure 1). The demographics of downtown San Francisco in comparison to the surrounding area may explain the distribution of service requests. For example, the majority of households with children live in the surrounding area associated with fewer requests, which may be due to the nature of the transportation-related requests that are used in this study. Similarly, those with at least a high school education are highly concentrated outside of the downtown district. These geographic hotspots warrant further analysis of San Francisco using less geographically biased 311 service requests which may produce more informative results for local governments.

One of the similarities across all three cities was the negative relationship between family structure and 311 requests. This relationship between family structure and 311 requests may be picking up the effect of differences in residential neighborhood infrastructure. For example, residential neighborhoods which are more suitable for families may be in areas with fewer parking meters and thus fewer parking meter problems than a high rise in the center of a city. Future research should work to incorporate the distribution of these types of infrastructure throughout the cities of interest.

In addition, it is interesting to note the contradictions and similarities across cities. San Francisco and New York City experienced almost an opposite effect in terms of age, while the results from New York City and Washington DC followed a similar pattern in terms of the direction of the association. This holds true for age, gender, race and ethnicity, and family structure. These results may have important spatial dimensions which are not discussed in this paper. Future research should also addresses how space and interactions across space within the city work to reinforce differential levels of participation in 311 and other government services.

Conclusion

The third wave of e-government promises increased access and greater transparency; but, the cost of ICTs may be reflected in the growing divide between those who can and those who cannot reap the benefits. While disparities were found in all three cities, there are possibilities for potential solutions. The creation and dissemination of VGI data by citizens not only provides a means to hold local institutions accountable, but also provides governments with the data to evaluate and improve the distribution of municipal services within their respective locations.

At the same time, discussions of the possibilities for VGI in e-government should also be coupled with a recognition of the newness of these types of information. The term "neogeography" has been suggested as problematic in terms of framing these new technologies associated with 311 and other new avenues of e-government (Leszczynski, 2014). In a way, this terminology has allowed technologies, such as 311 and others situated within the Geoweb or based on VGI to escape criticism based on their inherent "newness" (Leszczynski, 2014). Care should be taken to avoid viewing these technologies as a sort of "catch-all" for solving citizen issues, when in some instances these services can truly be a band-aid solution that continues to obscure and opt out certain populations and perspectives.

These results obtained using VGI reaffirm the conclusions reached in previous survey-based studies that call on municipalities to decrease intra-urban inequalities in access to public services. User-generated data, specifically VGI, maintains an inherent value for purposes of municipal planning and policy analysis, as the sheer volume of data in an area can be relevant in terms of residents' participation in local governance and awareness of municipal services. By identifying demographic groups with unequal access to the benefits of e-government services, local governments have the ability to target future policies and initiatives to narrow the digital divide and increase the population which can actively engage with these community-centered services.

The effects of new technologies on citizens' interaction with local institutions must continue to be critically evaluated. More information including data on methods of submission of service requests will inform future research. Further, socio-demographic groups are often clustered within regions that do not correspond to census geography. Incorporating a neighborhood unit of analysis may provide a more realistic assessment of socio-demographic status (Bell et al., 2013).

The benefits of 311 services are clear; yet, the way in which governments choose to use and implement the data (or lack of data) informs the success or failure of e-government. Further research which delves into the mechanisms behind why citizens choose to participate in 311 services will build off of this research and further explore the demography of active participants in 311 services.

These results indicate that certain areas differentially participate in 311 services. This has important implications for how certain populations, identified with our analysis, may be excluded from the benefits of 311. These benefits include both the direct impacts of improved transportation infrastructure on daily life, and also the ability to participate in the community and social capital building processes which occur through engaging in this form of e-government.

Bibliography

M. Asgarkhani, "The Reality of Social Inclusion Through Digital Government," *Journal of Technology in Human Services* 25 (2007) 127–146.

J. Baird, R. Zelin, and Q. Booker, "Is there a "Digital Divide" in the Provision of E-Government Services at the County Level in the United States?," *Journal of Legal, Ethical and Regulatory Issues* 15 (2012) 93–104.

F. Bélanger and L. Carter, "The Impact of the Digital Divide on E-Government Use," *Communications of the ACM* 52: 4 (2009) 132–135.

S. Bell, K. Wilson, L. Bissonnette and T. Shah, "Access to Primary Health Care: Does Neighborhood of Residence Matter?," *Annals of the Association of American Geographers* 103 (2013) 85–105.

E. Berman, "Dealing with Cynical Citizens," *Public Administration Review* 57: 2 (1997) 105–112.

CCSF, "About 311." (2012) *San Francisco 311*. City and County of San Francisco. <http://www.sf311.org/index.aspx?page=5> Accessed October 3, 2012.

J. Cinnamon and N. Schuurman, "Confronting the Data-Divide in a Time of Spatial Turns and Volunteered Geographic Information," *Geojournal* 78 (2012) 657–674.

M. Crutcher and M. Zook, "Placemarks and Waterlines: Racialized Cyberscapes in Post-Katrina Google Earth," *Geoforum* 40 (2009) 523–534.

DC, "311 Online," (2012) District of Columbia <311.dc.gov> Accessed December 9, 2012.

A. Dugdale, et al., "Accessing E-Government: Challenges for Citizens and Organizations," *International Review of Administrative Sciences* 71: 1 (2005) 109–118.

E-Government Act of 2002, Pub. L. No. 107–347, §2, 116 Stat. 2901 (Washington D.C.: Government Printing Office, 2002).

N. Elbahnasawy, "E-Government, Internet Adoption, and Corruption: An Empirical Investigation," *World Development* 57 (2014) 114–126.

S. Elwood, "Geographic Information Science: Emerging Research on the Societal Implications of the Geospatial Web," *Progress in Human Geography* 34 (2010) 349–357.

S. Elwood, M. Goodchild, and D. Sui, "Researching Volunteered Geographic Information: Spatial Data, Geographic Research, and New Social Practice," *Annals of the Association of American Geographers* 102 (2012) 571–590.

J. Evans-Cowley, and M. Conroy, "The Growth of E-Government in Municipal Planning," *Journal of Urban Technology* 13: 1 (2006) 81–107.

M. Gilbert et al., "Theorizing the Digital Divide: Information and Communication Technology Use Frameworks among Poor Women Using a Telemedicine System," *Geoforum* 39: 2 (2008) 912–925.

M. Goodchild, "Citizens as Sensors: the World of Volunteered Geography," *Geojournal* 69 (2007) 211–221.

T. Hall and J. Owens, "The Digital Divide and E-Government Services," In E. Estevez and M. Janssen, Eds., *Proceedings of the 5th International Conference on Theory and Practice of Electronic Governance* (New York: Association for Computing Machinery, 2011) 37–44.

K. Hampton, and B. Wellman, "Neighboring in Netville: How the Internet Supports Community and Social Capital in a Wired Suburb," *City & Community* 2: 4 (2003) 277–311.

P. Johnson and R. Sieber, "Motivations Driving Government Adoption of the Geoweb," *GeoJournal* 77 (2012) 677–680.

P. Johnson and R. Sieber, "Situating the Adoption of VGI by Government," in D. Sui, S. Elwood and M. Goodchild, eds., *Crowdsourcing Geographic Knowledge: Volunteered Geographic Information (VGI) in Theory and Practice* (New York: Springer Science & Business Media Dordrecht, 2013) 65–81.

A. Leszczynski, "On the Neo in Neogeography," *Annals of the Association of American Geographers* 104: 1 (2014) 60–79.

D. Maguire & P. Longley, "The Emergence of Geoportals and Their Role in Spatial Data Infrastructures," *Computers, Environment and Urban Systems* 29: 1 (2005) 3–14.

NCR, "The New Laboratories of Democracy. Part three: Potholes and PDAs," *National Civic Review* 98 (2009) 15–20. doi: 10.1002/ncr.247

NYC311, Department of Information Technology and Telecom. The City of New York. Web. 28 Mar (2014) <http://www1.nyc.gov/connect/applications.page> Accessed March 7th, 2014.

Open311.org, "GeoReport v2/Servers," (2012) <http://wiki.open311.org/GeoReport_v2/Servers> Accessed November 7, 2012.

SF311, San Francisco 24×7 Service Center. The City of San Francisco, CA (2014) <http://sf311.org/index.aspx?page=797> Accessed March 7th, 2014.

R. Schwester, T. Carrizales, and M. Holzer, "An Examination of the Municipal 311 System," *International Journal of Organization Theory and Behavior* 12 (2009) 218–236.

M. Stephens, "Gender and the Geoweb: Divisions in the Production of User-Generated Cartographic Information," *GeoJournal* 78 (2013) 981–996. DOI: 10.1007/s10708-013-9492-Z.

J. Thomas and G. Streib, "The New Face of Government: Citizen-Initiated Contacts in the Era of E-Government," *Journal of Public Administration Research and Theory* 13 (2003) 83–102.

J. Thomas, "Creating a Citizen-Friendly City Hall: An Evaluation of the Chattanooga 311 Innovations," in *The Proceedings of The International Conference on Engaging Communities*, eds., D. Gardiner and K. Scott (Brisbane, Australia: Queensland Department of Main Roads, 2005), 1–14.

A. Turner, *Introduction to Neogeography* (Sebastopol, CA: O'Reilly Media, 2006).

U. S. Census Bureau, *American Community Survey, 5-year Estimates: San Francisco, C.A.* (U.S. Census Bureau, 2011c) <http://factfinder2.census.gov/> Accessed October 20, 2012.

U. S. Census Bureau, *Profile of General Population and Housing Characteristics: San Francisco, C.A.* (U.S. Census Bureau, 2010a) <http://factfinder2.census.gov/> Accessed October 20, 2012.

U. S. Census Bureau, *Profile of General Population and Housing Characteristics: Washington, D.C.* (U.S. Census Bureau, 2010b) <http://factfinder2.census.gov/> Accessed October 20, 2012.

U. S. Census Bureau, *Profile of General Population and Housing Characteristics: New York City, N.Y.* (U.S. Census Bureau, 2010c) <http://factfinder2.census.gov/> Accessed October 20, 2012.

U. S. Census Bureau, *American Community Survey, 5-year Estimates: Washington D.C.* (U.S. Census Bureau, 2011a) <http://factfinder2.census.gov/> Accessed October 20, 2012.

U. S. Census Bureau, *American Community Survey, 5-year Estimates: New York City, N.Y.* (U.S. Census Bureau, 2011b) <http://factfinder2.census.gov/> Accessed October 20, 2012.

L. Van Aerschot and N. Rodousakis, "The Link Between Socioeconomic Background and Internet Use: Barriers Faced by Low Socio-economic Status Groups and Possible Solutions," *Innovation: the European Journal of Social Science Research* 21 (2008) 317–351.

T. Wolhers, "The Digital World of Local Government: A Comparative Analysis of the United States and Germany," *Journal of Information Technology* 6 (2009) 126–0.

Does Anything Ever Happen Around Here? Assessing the Online Information Landscape for Local Events

Claudia López, Brian Butler, and Peter Brusilovsky

ABSTRACT *Local events foster community pride, cohesion, and community attachment. Keeping residents informed about the existence of local events is necessary to reach events' targeted audiences and realize their positive consequences. This article reports on an initial study of the online event information landscape of neighborhoods in a mid-sized US city. Our results show that the event information landscape is highly fragmented, decentralized, and has low rates of duplication. This creates challenges for residents looking for event information and for event organizers and technology developers seeking to provide timely information about events.*

Introduction

Cities and neighborhoods host many kinds of events. Non-profits run festivals, workshops, and fundraising events; arts and entertainment organizations arrange performances and shows; city governments run meetings, organize celebrations, and offer seasonal activities. Local events have economic and social impacts (Sherwood, 2007; Getz, 2010). Events generate economic costs and revenue (Daniels and Norman, 2003), foster community cohesiveness (Gursoy et al., 2004), encourage pride and attachment (Getz, 2010), reflect a sense of community (Derrett, 2003), and facilitate interaction among community members (Misener and Mason, 2006).

Community member awareness of events is an important, but often overlooked, precondition for achieving any of the desired effects of community events. While providing information about an event does not ensure actual attendance and success, disseminating event information is one of three key components of effective event management (the other ones are event provision and event financing) (Giesecke, 2011). Failing to support the seemingly mundane activity of distributing event information can significantly reduce the impact of efforts to plan and run events. As a result, communities have long created and maintained infrastructures that facilitate dissemination of information about past, current, and future events. Historically, bulletin boards, newsletters, and traditional media have all been used to provide information about local events. Originating from event sponsors, organizers, and third parties (e.g., reporters or newsletter editors), materials in these traditional channels have provided information for those seeking to participate in or support events.

However, changes in resident mobility, media business models, and technology have led to concerns about developing weaknesses in local communities (Wellman, 2001), lower civic participation (Putman, 2000), and changes to traditional local information channels (Gurstein, 1999). Suburbanization and separation of residential and commercial facilities have led to fewer shared community spaces (Putman, 2000), which in turn undermines the creation of shared physical information spaces. Local media outlets face significant economic challenges and national media organizations are less sensitive to local communities' needs. The Web has also reshaped local information landscapes, allowing individuals to share and access information "anywhere." Sites operating on a national or global level, such as Metromix[1] and Eventful,[2] have the potential to become sources of local event information. At the same time, local organizations can run their own sites to provide this kind of information.

Despite the potential of local events to strengthen communities and the undergoing fundamental changes in event information infrastructures, critical questions remain about dissemination of local event information. Where do local events get publicized online? How do different types of organizations and web sites differ in their coverage of local events? Compared to traditional media, does the Web and social media expand access to and enhance diffusion of local event information?

To address these questions about the changing nature of local event information sources, this paper examines the online event information landscapes of four neighborhoods in Pittsburgh, PA, a mid-size US city. We begin with a consideration of related work about local events, event management, and technology for supporting community-information sharing. We then describe the methods used to select relevant local and mass media sites and collect event information during the nine-month longitudinal study. This is followed by analysis and empirical findings that indicate that the event information infrastructures in these communities are highly fragmented and heterogeneous. We then conclude with limitations of this study and a discussion on the implications of the findings for software developers who seek to increase awareness about local events and information scientists who aim to understand and enhance local information availability.

Related Work

Local events play an important role in community life. Significant time, effort, and money go into planning, promoting, and running local events. Yet despite this, little attention has been given to understanding the nature of event information and event information infrastructures within communities. This section summarizes prior research documenting the importance of local events in community life and describing the means used to propagate and find event information.

Local Events

Events have a positive impact on the quality of life of a community (Delamere et al., 2001; Sherwood, 2007; Kantar-Media, 2013). Although events may have some negative consequences for some residents, such as the disruption of normal routines and increased levels of noise, litter, and traffic, there is a general consensus that the social benefits of local events are often greater than the associated costs (Arcodia and Whitford, 2006).

At the individual level, events provide opportunities for people to learn new things, to be exposed to different cultural experiences, and to practice new activities (Delamere et al., 2001). Youth volunteers in sports events report individual benefits such as augmented social connections (Kay and Bradbury, 2009). Festivals and special local events create opportunities for leisure (Getz and Frisby, 1991). Participation in recreational events is associated with increased subjective perceptions of personal well-being (Lloyd and Auld, 2002; Brajsa-Zganec et al., 2011).

Local events also have consequences for the whole community and for residents' perceptions about their communities. In sports events, for example, social interaction among individuals who participate, plan, and volunteer can create new social networks, increasing community social capital (Misener and Mason, 2006). Similarly, festival attendance can positively affect the development of various forms of social capital in a community (Arcodia and Whitford, 2006). Attending music festivals engenders an increased perception of friendliness and trust among strangers attending the same event and strengthens current social relationships among attendees. However, it does not enable the creation of enduring connections with previously unrelated attendees (Wilks, 2011). Researchers have also found that events can foster community cohesiveness (Gursoy et al., 2004). Having strong group relationships is associated with higher levels of satisfaction within small and mid-sized communities (Goudy, 1977). Increased community satisfaction and attachment, in turn, is correlated with a higher quality of life among community members (Theodori, 2001; Misener and Mason, 2006).

Events have been also associated, both empirically and aspirationally, with residents having more community pride and community attachment (Delamere et al., 2001; Getz, 2010). Evidence of increased civic pride has been found when evaluating large-scale events (Waitt, 2001; Ntloko and Swart, 2008). Urban governments often perceive their sport events strategies as a way to increase and sustain community pride (Misener and Mason, 2006). Non-profits and government entities that organize festivals report that increasing community pride/spirits is one of the main reasons to stage such events (Mayfield and Crompton, 1995).

Local Event Information

Although organizing successful community events remains more of an art than a science, prior work has identified three key components of effective event management: event information, financing, and provision (Giesecke, 2011). Within this model dissemination of event information is a necessary (but not sufficient) condition for event success. Financial resources and activity coordination are critical, but without community members being aware of an event, there will be no participants, no activity, and no positive impacts. For this reason, both local organizations and individuals make special efforts to disseminate and find information about local events. Event organizers, community organizations, and venue managers actively work to disseminate information about current and future events. Beyond the direct stakeholders are many others, such as, event calendar providers, event food providers, ticket sellers, media sales organizations, and media content providers, who play a role in disseminating information about events (Giesecke, 2011).

Individuals also spend significant amounts of time and effort intentionally seeking information about local events. Fifty-seven percent of Americans report that they follow news about communities and neighborhood events, such as parades or block parties; 60 percent of people follow news about local arts and cultural events, such as concerts, plays, and museums exhibitions; and 42 percent get information about local government activities, such as council meetings, hearings and local trials (Rosenstiel et al., 2011). In the UK, 27 percent of residents consume local news to get information about community events and 22 percent want to get news about local arts and cultural events (Kantar-Media, 2013). Local events are also a common topic in neighborhood Facebook groups (López and Butler, 2013).

Visitors to local events report having used a range of information sources including word of mouth, brochures, posters, newspapers, radio, TV, and the Internet (Smith, 2007), with word of mouth often being reported as the most popular source (Smith, 2008). Traditional media such as TV, radio, and newspapers are also common sources of events information, especially for older people. The Internet has a secondary role in providing information about local events, but it is increasingly important for younger people and visitors living more than 50 miles away from the event location (Lee and Kim, 2011). Given the importance of word of mouth (Smith, 2007), the new capabilities provided by the Web and social media have the potential to significantly change local event information landscapes and practices. However, it is still unclear how the emergence of new technologies and infrastructure will affect the way that information about local events is disseminated.

Diversity and Distribution of Local Events: A Baseline

Although the idea of local events being important is generally accepted, their diversity and distribution within neighborhoods and communities have not been systematically examined. Basic questions about event types, frequency, geographic distribution, and sponsorship are not well addressed, leaving community system developers, planners, leaders, and researchers to rely on anecdotal evidence and personal impressions as the basis for interface, information, and technology choices. In this section we will examine data from a prominent source (the newspaper of record in the focal communities) to establish a baseline for the number, types, and distribution of local events. We will then reference this baseline to begin to understand how the Web and social media have changed the local event information landscape.

Traditional media have long been important sources of information about local events, and local newspapers are investing serious effort in maintaining and expanding this aspect of their work in the age of online information. For example, the *Pittsburgh Post-Gazette*,[3] one of the main local newspapers and the newspaper of record in Pittsburgh, provides an online Events section on its web site that advertises local events. Submitting information about an event to this section is free, but the event information is subject to a moderation process. The newspaper's staff decides what events are eventually advertised online. Major local newspapers have a long tradition of gathering and disseminating information about local events and as a result remain an important source of event information for people in many communities. For this reason, data from this major local newspaper provide a baseline for understanding the scope and diversity of local events and the information available about them.

The baseline community event dataset for this study contains information about all events posted in the Events section of the *Post-Gazette*'s web site from the end of June 2011 until March 2012. The data were acquired directly from the staff of the *Post-Gazette*, who extracted it from the newspaper's content management system. It included information about 2,848 events during a nine month period, or more than 10 events per day on average. While this data may not capture all of the events occurring in this urban environment, they are sufficient to demonstrate that local events are not infrequent occurrences, but rather a regular, ongoing element of the community.

Community events were hosted in 719 different venues. Ninety-eight percent of those events were associated with a specific neighborhood and a total of 132 different neighborhoods were referenced. The City of Pittsburgh officially has 89 neighborhoods. The remaining 43 neighborhoods mentioned are located in towns, counties, and regions near Pittsburgh. Events were announced in 49 of the neighborhoods in Pittsburgh (55 percent). These neighborhoods are uniformly distributed throughout the city with no discernable pattern of inclusion/exclusion related to geography.

Events were unequally distributed across neighborhoods. (See Figure 1.) Each neighborhood had an average of 21 events, but the number of events in a neighborhood ranged from 1 to 225. A majority of the neighborhoods (58 percent, 77 neighborhoods) had fewer than 10 events. Slightly more than 15 percent (24 neighborhoods) hosted between 10 and 20 events. Only 9 percent (12 neighborhoods) had more than 50 events.

Event venues were also unevenly spread among neighborhoods (See Figure 1). Seven hundred three venues were associated with a neighborhood. On average, each neighborhood had five venues, but more than 60 percent (87 neighborhoods) had fewer than five venues. Only eight neighborhoods were associated with more than 20 event venues. Additionally, while more than half of the venues hosted only one event, the most active venue was responsible for 78 events. Thus, while there were not strong geographical biases in which neighborhoods have events, there was significant inequality in the number of events and event venues across neighborhoods.

The types of events announced also varied significantly. As part of the moderation process, event submitters and *Post-Gazette* staff categorize each event. While many different types of events are present, the frequency of events in each category was not evenly distributed (See Figure 2). Charities, Concerts

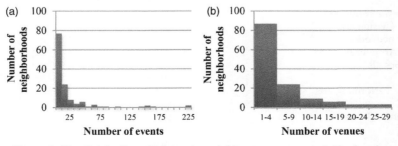

Figure 1: The distribution of (a) events and (b) venues among neighborhoods.

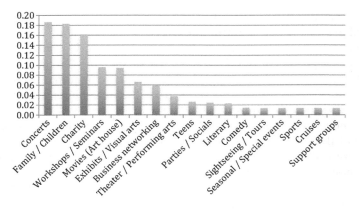

Figure 2: Frequency of community event types.

and Family/Children events were the most popular with each of them accounting for more than 16 percent of the total number of events. However, events such as Support Groups for Adults, Seasonal/Special Events, and Cruises were much less common.

The non-uniform allocation of community events and event types was further confirmed by examining the distribution of events in each category by neighborhood (See Table 1).[4] Although the average values resemble the distribution shown in Figure 2, the standard deviation values are all larger than averages, indicating that the proportions in each category varied widely among the neighborhoods.

Our analysis of the baseline data from a major local newspaper indicates that community events are a frequent, ubiquitous aspect of this urban environment. There are more events than any one person could possibly participate in (or even read about) and they cover a range of audiences (e.g., teens, family/children, adults) and purposes (e.g., arts-related events, charities, business networking). Yet, while the sheer volume and diversity of events within the city as a whole is high, the distribution is uneven. Neighborhoods greatly differ in their numbers of events and venues. Many of them account for few events and only a few are respon-

Table 1: Proportion of event types by neighborhood.

	Average	Std. dev.
Charity	0.31	0.32
Family / Children	0.19	0.35
Concerts	0.12	0.22
Workshops / Seminars	0.10	0.19
Exhibits / Visual arts	0.05	0.15
Business networking	0.04	0.10
Movies (Art house)	0.03	0.13
Parties/Socials	0.03	0.09
Teens	0.03	0.11
Theater / Performing arts	0.03	0.11
Comedy	0.02	0.12
Sightseeing / Tours	0.02	0.09
Literary	0.01	0.04
Sports	0.01	0.06

sible for a large share of the total number of events. Moreover, neighborhoods vary considerably in their proportions of different kinds of events. Combined, these features of local events present individuals with a complex information management problem. If they chose to rely on citywide information sources they are likely to be overwhelmed by the volume. Yet, if they rely on immediate, simplistic neighborhood-focused filters they are likely to miss relevant events. It is this problem that successful local event information infrastructures must help individuals, organizations, and communities solve.

Online Sources of Local Event Information

The nature of local events creates significant opportunities and challenges for organizers and local information providers seeking to use the Internet to reach the right audience. The Web enables them to provide information about events through online outlets such as social media, traditional media, their own, and their partners' web sites. Organizers and information providers need to make decisions about how to use the available channels to best disseminate their event data without getting lost in huge streams of data that can cause information overload for residents. Community residents also play a role in dissemination of local events information when they choose to share it through social media sites. As a result, making decisions about where and how to distribute information about local events requires significant expertise and effort, which can vary among different kinds of event organizers and information providers.

Underlying decisions about local event information management are assumptions about how the online systems for disseminating event information currently function. Event planners and communications professionals make assumptions about what sources typically have information about different events and types of events. Community and organization leaders who decide whether and how to allocate resources for technology, development, and staffing make assumptions about how these resources will affect the community. Individual users make assumptions about the comprehensiveness and completeness of different online sources of local event information. Researchers make assumptions about the availability and quality of information about local events in different contexts. Yet, in spite of the importance of these assumptions, there is little or no systematic data available about the nature and structure of neighborhood-level event information infrastructures.

To begin addressing this gap, we gathered data from a sample of sites associated with four Pittsburgh neighborhoods: Bloomfield, East Liberty, Highland Park, and Squirrel Hill.[5] The selected neighborhoods are located in the eastern side of Pittsburgh. They vary with respect to population, age demographics, and median income (See Table 2).

Table 2: Sampled neighborhood demographics.

Neighborhood	Population	% over 60	Median income
Bloomfield	8,442	19.96	31,803
East Liberty	5,869	21.97	23,683
Highland Park	6,395	16.37	63,394
Squirrel Hill (North)	11,363	15.92	86,508

Bloomfield is a middle-class neighborhood that is known as Pittsburgh's Little Italy. Its diverse population includes college students, European immigrant, and African American families. Bloomfield has an active business district with many local restaurants and businesses and few small franchised establishments. This gives the neighborhood a local atmosphere that seems to resemble the close-knit and proud character of its community.

East Liberty is currently a neighborhood with majority African-American population. Prior to the 1960s, East Liberty was a major commercial center within Pittsburgh. However, infrastructure changes implemented as part of urban redevelopment efforts led to a decline in commercial activity and deterioration of the neighborhood's reputation. Recent efforts have succeeded at bringing large retail chain stores, new restaurants, and a renovated branch of the city library to East Liberty, which has served to reestablish the neighborhood's reputation as a thriving commercial and residential neighborhood.

Highland Park has a small and racially diverse population. It is predominantly a residential neighborhood that has a much higher median income than the aforementioned neighborhoods. This neighborhood is built around a large city park and the Pittsburgh Zoo. Recently, a very small business district has emerged to provide its residents with a small grocery store and a few local restaurants. Nevertheless, Highland Park is mostly known as a residential area.

Finally, Squirrel Hill is the largest and wealthiest neighborhood in our sample. A well-established Jewish community and many undergraduate and graduate students are distinctive features of its population. Similar to Bloomfield, it has an active business district that provides its residents with many services within walking distance of their homes. This business district includes local and franchised establishments in similar proportion. It also hosts a large, prominently located branch of the city library. Furthermore, this neighborhood also contains two city parks and is close to several universities, making it attractive for families and students.

Although our sampled neighborhoods differ in several ways, examination of the baseline community event data (described above) indicates that these four neighborhoods are exemplars of average, moderately active, communities with respect to the number and types of events that they host.[6]

To identify online information sources of event information associated with each neighborhood, we conducted Google searches using the neighborhood's name and "Pittsburgh" as the search terms. We conducted additional Google searches by alternatively adding the nouns "event," "happening," and "calendar," which are common in event pages, to the initial search string. For each search, the first 20 search results were examined and the top 10 search results that met the sampling requirements were recorded.[7] The sampling requirements excluded sponsored pages, images, maps, news, and Wikipedia pages. Each page was also reviewed to identify direct links to other pages that advertise local events. The purpose of this process was to identify web sites that a community resident might reasonably be expected to find and/or consult when looking for information about events happening in their neighborhood.

The sampling procedure identified a wide variety of sites run by many different organizations (See Table 3). Using the description of the sites' mission or goals, we categorized the sites into the following ten groups: Arts, Community, Entertainment, Government, Library, Parks and Zoo, Religious, Web information provider, and Traditional media. The resulting sample

Table 3: Sampled pages and sites.

Site Type	# Pages Sampled	# Sites Selected	# Active event sites
Art	1	1	1
Community	8	8	3
Entertainment	2	2	2
Government	2	1	1
Library	2	1	1
Other	1	1	0
Parks & Zoo	3	2	2
Religious	3	3	3
Web info provider	15	12	4
Traditional media	8	4	3
Total	45	35	19

included 45 pages from 35 different sites. Each arts-related, community, entertainment, and religious organizations' page belonged to a different web site. The two government pages were part of the same site (i.e., a common base URL), but were run by different agencies. The two library pages were from different branches of the same institution. Three pages were associated with two organizations associated with the city parks and the zoo. Fifteen pages were part of 12 web information providers that advertise events, restaurants, and other local businesses. Eight pages were related to four traditional media such as TV channels and newspapers. Overall, there were 35 unique sites in the sample of 45 neighborhood-specific event information pages.

The sampled sites were each reviewed to ensure that they represented potential sources of information about events in the targeted neighborhoods. As noted above, the *Pittsburgh Post-Gazette* maintains a page for every neighborhood, which contains information about local events. While the *Post-Gazette* site was consistently "discovered" when sampling sites for each neighborhood, its status as a long-time, widely accepted local information source led us to treat it as a special baseline case and not as a representative member of the sample. Review of the remaining 34 sites that were initially selected revealed that four sites[8] contained information about the neighborhoods' restaurants, news, and books but no information about events. In the process of collecting data from the remaining 30 sites (between June 2011 and March 2012), 11 more sites were dropped from the sample because they did not provide any new information about local events. Exclusion of these sites resulted in a final sample of 19 distinct sites that had provided information about local events.

While the final composition of the site sample is methodologically significant, it also provides an initial characterization of the structure of the local event information landscape. Different types of organizations are more (or less) likely to provide local event information on their web sites (See Table 3). Eight community organizations claimed to advertise events; however, only three of them provided new information about events during the nine-month observation period. In the case of web information providers that meant to display information about events, only four out of nine provided descriptions of new events, and all of them were social media sites that relied on users to provide information about local events.

Table 4: Active event information sites by resource model.

Resources model of sites	# Sites for events	# Sites without current events
For-profit	14	5
Non-profit	12	6
Government	1	0
Religious	3	0

Organizations running sites that sought to provide event information also differed with respect to their resource models (See Table 4). Fourteen sites belonged to for-profit organizations, 12 sites were run by non-profit organizations, and the remaining four were managed by city government and religious institutions. Somewhat unexpectedly, sites that sought, but failed, to provide local event information were split almost evenly between for-profit and non-profit organizations.

Slightly more than half of the sites that claimed to provide information about events (16 of 30) were focused on a specific neighborhood. The remaining 14 sites had a broader geographic scope such as city or countrywide. These sites provided information about local events in specific pages for particular neighborhoods. Sites that failed to have an active stream of new information about local events were equally distributed with respect to geographic scope, with 35–40 percent of each level having no new event information during the observation period.

Together these results suggest that there is a significant gap between organizations' interest in providing local event information and their ability to do so on a regular basis. Only 63 percent of the sites (19 out of 30) that claimed to provide information about local events actually managed to have a minimally active stream of event information. This reflects a system maintenance problem in a considerable number of the sampled sites. While a number of organizations could make a one-time investment to set up a web site with an event section, only a fraction of them could provide the resources needed (e.g., staff or volunteer content providers) to keep this section up to date. Yet, the failure to achieve this basic goal was not simply explained in terms of organizational mission, resource model, or geographic focus.

Data Analysis of Local Events Information

Data were collected from the identified sites by visiting them once a week for nine months between the end of June 2011 and March 2012. Each time a site was visited, event pages (identified in the sampling process described above) were examined and any new events were identified. For each new event a title, description, time and date, location (venue), URL, and sponsoring organization was recorded. If any of these elements were not present on the primary site, available links were followed to find additional information. In the absence of explicit links to additional information a Google search was performed to find necessary event information.

Additional information was collected about each event to support description and analysis of the overall structure of the local event information landscape. The date and site where each event was first identified was recorded. If an event was identified on more than one site, all sites were recorded. To allow for direct comparison of each site with the baseline source, the presence (or absence) of each event in the *Post-Gazette* web site was also determined and recorded. Examples of the event coding are shown in the Appendix. The result of this process was a dataset that contained information about 414 events, which were found on one or more of the 19 sampled sites between the end of June 2011 and March 2012.

What Kinds of Events Get Posted Online?

The baseline data from the *Post-Gazette* and the sample of local events collected from the other online event information sources contain different types of local events. In the *Post-Gazette* data, concerts, events for family/children, and charities were the more frequent kind of events across all neighborhoods (See Figure 3). Although concerts were also the most popular event type in the data collected from local sites, the proportion was much higher than in the *Post-Gazette* (32 percent vs. 19 percent). Charity events were very rarely announced on our sampled sites (2 percent) even though they comprised 16 percent of the events in the *Post-Gazette*. Another important difference is related to parties and socials events. The sampled local event information sources announced a large number of social events such as community days, meetings for neighbors, and volunteer work days that were rarely listed as events in the Events section in the *Post-Gazette*. This event type comprised 19 percent of the events in the collected data, a significantly greater proportion than found in the *Post-Gazette* (2 percent).

To determine if this variation is due to differences in the neighborhood or in the information sources, we examined the events from the *Post-Gazette* that were explicitly associated with one of the four target neighborhoods. Most significantly, the baseline local newspaper had information about a considerably smaller set of events than the overall event information infrastructure. The *Post-Gazette* site contained only 159 events for the sampled neighborhoods. The rates for particular types of events also differed significantly between the two samples (See Figure 4). For example, the *Post-Gazette* had only19 concerts for the selected neighborhoods, while other online information sources included 134. The local sites announced many concerts hosted in small entertainment venues located in these neighborhoods, most of which were not advertised in the citywide traditional media. To a lesser extent, the pattern was also found for events for family and children's

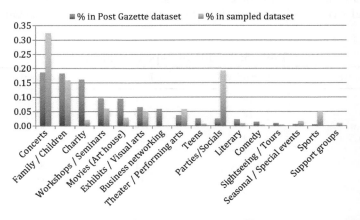

Figure 3: Event type proportions—*Post Gazette* (citywide) and neighborhood sites.

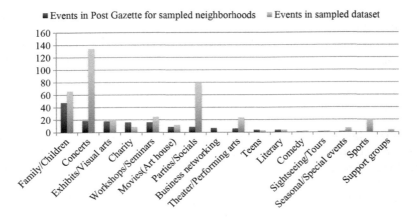

Figure 4: Event type counts—*Post-Gazette* (neighborhoods) and neighborhood sites.

events, workshops/seminars, social events, theater/performing arts events, seasonal special events, and sport events.

Together these results suggest that, while the traditional citywide paper of record may have greater visibility and longer history, the types and number of events found in it can differ significantly from what is available in other local online sites.

Who Organizes Local Events?

The 414 collected events were planned by 79 different organizations. On average, a sponsoring organization arranged 5.24 local events during the observation period. Similar to the general patterns found in the baseline dataset, the number of events per organization followed a long tail distribution with 67 percent (53) of the sponsors organizing only one event and 20 percent (16) of the organizations running between two and six events. The remaining 13 percent (10) of the organizers each offered between 10 and 55 events.

Sponsors' events varied significantly with respect to their visibility in the online event information sources (See Table 5). Among the institutions that organized local events, nine entertainment organizations such as restaurants, bars,

Table 5: Events by type of organizer.

Type of organizer	# Organizers	# Events	% of total	Mean
Arts	28	51	.12	1.82
Community	17	40	.10	2.35
Entertainment	9	124	.30	13.78
Government	4	39	.09	9.75
Library	1	47	.11	47.00
Museum	1	1	.00	1.00
Other	10	14	.03	1.40
Parks & Zoo	3	72	.17	24.00
Religious	6	26	.06	4.33
Total	79	414	1	5.24

and concert promoters were responsible for 30 percent (124) of the events. Three organizations related to city parks and the zoo organized 17 percent, and 28 arts-related organizations, including art galleries and theaters, offered 12 percent of the local events. The two branches of the city library organized 11 percent of the identified events. Seventeen community organizations ran 40 events (10 percent of the total). The city councils of Pittsburgh and other three nearby cities were the organizers of 9 percent of the events. Six religious institutions hosted 6 percent and other organizations such as fitness centers, cemeteries, and small businesses organized 3 percent of the events.

Interestingly, our sample included only one event organized by a museum. Although the city has several museums near the studied neighborhoods, the sampled online sources of local event information did not mention events sponsored by these organizations. Although our study cannot explain the reasons behind this observation, it is possible that museums' events are not targeted to specific neighborhoods but rather target a citywide audience. This would lead museums to use broadly targeted channels to disseminate information about their events. In contrast, the library branches and the organizations related to the parks and zoo were some of the most prolific local event organizers with an average of 20 events each. The entertainment-focused organization offered around 13 events per institution, while arts organizations were individually less prominent users of the local event information sources with less than two events each. Overall, this suggests that organizations vary significantly both with respect to how many events they organize and the degree to which they use neighborhood information sources to propagate information about them.

Who Advertises Local Events? Whose Events Do They Promote?

As noted above, many organizations that clearly intend to use their web sites as sources of information about local events fail to achieve even a minimum level of activity. Organizations seeking to provide local event information can do so by using the sites to promote both their own events and those sponsored by other organizations. Of the 19 event information sites identified in our sample, 13 sites were owned by *event organizers*. The remaining six were *event-dissemination sites* that provided information about other organizations' events and did not sponsor any of the identified local events. The 13 event organizers' sites accounted for 73 percent of the events ($n = 302$ events) averaging 23 events each. These sites also had information about 55 events that were arranged by the other 26 institutions.

The six event-dissemination sites included three web sites associated with local traditional media and three social media sites. Traditional media sites in our sample (excluding the *Post-Gazette*) reported 21 percent (88) of the sampled events, while social media sites included information about 13 percent (53). Together, traditional and social media provided information about events from 52 different event organizers, though only 14 of the event organizers were present in both traditional and social media. Traditional media covered events of 21 organizations that social media did not. In turn, 17 organizations that advertised their events in social media did not appear on traditional media sites. Except for government organizations, which always use traditional media and never appeared on social media sites, there was no clear pattern of which types of event organizers' events were associated with which type of event information site.

The degree to which events and event organizers crossed over category boundaries also varied (See Table 6). Arts and community organizations' events appeared on almost all types of sites. Except for government sites, most of the sites publicized events from at least one of the 28 arts-related organizations. However, this crossover does not appear to be reciprocated, with all but the arts-related sites announcing community organizations' events. Religious organizations and city parks and the zoo used only traditional and social media sites. The library branches' events appeared on only one community organization's site.

In general, traditional and social media sites had information about events from the broadest range of organizations. However, traditional and social media did not significantly differ from one another with respect to types or number of organizations for which they promoted events. Among the rest of the sampled sites, it is notable that while community organizations played a role as information propagators by advertising events of several other kinds of organizations, the library branches advertised only a small number of arts and community organizations' events.

Different strategies for using the available event information sources and/or providing information about others' local events are also reflected in the distribution of events across the different types of sites (See Table 7).

Overall, traditional media had a broader coverage of events than social media for all kinds of organizers. A larger proportion of the arts organizations' events was found in traditional media web sites (63 percent) than in social media sites (55 percent). Traditional media sites also had information about approximately a third of the events sponsored by entertainment and other organizations (e.g., coffee shops and other "third-places").

It is also notable that 44 percent of the government events were also advertised by the city parks organization, a community organization that was created as a public-private partnership with the Pittsburgh city government. The remaining types of event organizers did not have a significant proportion of their events present on other organizers' sites. Community organizations and the government sites tended to advertise slightly more of third-party events than the rest of the

Table 6: Number of sites that advertise third parties' events.

Event organizers	Arts	Community Organization	Entertainment Organization	Government	Library	Parks and zoo	Traditional media	Social media
Arts	1	2	1	0	1	1	13	18
Community	0	2	2	4	1	2	5	3
Entertainment	0	0	0	0	0	0	9	7
Government	0	0	0	1	0	2	1	0
Library	0	1	0	0	0	0	0	0
Museum	0	0	0	0	0	0	1	0
Other	0	3	0	1	0	0	5	4
Parks and zoo	0	3	0	1	0	0	1	1
Religious	0	0	0	0	0	0	3	2

Table 7: Volume and distribution of events—organizer type x site type.

Event Organizer Type	Arts	Community	Entertainment	Government	Library	Parks & zoo	Traditional media	Social media
Arts	1 (.02)	2 (.04)	1 (.02)	0 (.00)	1 (.02)	1 (.02)	32 (.63)	28 (.55)
Community	0 (.00)	3 (.08)	2 (.05)	4 (.10)	1 (.03)	3 (.08)	4 (.15)	4 (.10)
Entertainment	0 (.00)	0 (.00)	0 (.00)	0 (.00)	0 (.00)	0 (.00)	36 (.29)	13 (.10)
Government	0 (.00)	0 (.00)	0 (.00)	1 (.03)	0 (.00)	17 (.44)	1 (.03)	0 (.00)
Library	0 (.00)	1 (.02)	0 (.00)	0 (.00)	0 (.00)	0 (.00)	0 (.00)	0 (.00)
Museum	0 (.00)	0 (.00)	0 (.00)	0 (.00)	0 (.00)	0 (.00)	1 (1.00)	0 (.00)
Other	0 (.00)	3 (.21)	0 (.00)	2 (.14)	0 (.00)	0 (.00)	7 (.50)	3 (.21)
Parks & zoo	0 (.00)	6 (.08)	0 (.00)	6 (.08)	0 (.00)	0 (.00)	2 (.03)	1 (.01)
Religious	0 (.00)	0 (.00)	0 (.00)	0 (.00)	0 (.00)	0 (.00)	3 (.12)	3 (.12)

sites, while the city library branch did very little in promotion of others' events. This may reflect choices by the event organizers with respect to where and how they disseminate event information, or it may reflect choices by the organizations running the sites. In any case, these findings suggest that where and how local event information is provided is the result of a complex set of interdependent, distinct, and potentially idiosyncratic, organizational decisions—raising significant questions about how well the emergent system can be expected to operate as a coherent information infrastructure for a community. Does this event information infrastructure support all subpopulations equally well or are there particular types of events, audience, and venues that it works better for (and others for which it doesn't work well)? How does the organizational composition of a community's event information infrastructure relate to its coverage and information quality? Do organizations' choices about whether or not to participate in the event information infrastructure reflect the strengths and weakness of the current infrastructure and the needs of the community (or is it based solely on the perceived instrumental benefits for the organization)? In a centrally managed infrastructure controlled by single entity, designing a high quality, comprehensive, and fair event information infrastructure is largely a matter of systems design and implementation. In a decentralized infrastructure, such as the observed community event information infrastructure, those same issues can only be addressed indirectly requiring a much better understanding of how organizational choices, individual behavior, and information structures interact to affect the emergent system.

How Much Duplication Is There in the Local Event Information Infrastructure?

The effort required to create and maintain local event information, the number and diversity of organizations involved, and the potential for information overload lead to questions about the degree of redundancy in a community's event information infrastructure. One measure of this is the number of events that are announced on two or more sites in the community. By this measure, there is a surprisingly low level of redundancy of information about local events in the studied communities, with only 16 percent of the recorded events being listed on more

Table 8: Duplication rates by organizer type.

Type of organizer	Duplicated in sampled sites	Duplicated in *Post Gazette*	Non-duplicated events
Arts	16 (.31)	9 (.18)	31 (.61)
Community	1 (.03)	6 (.15)	33 (.83)
Entertainment	15 (.12)	2 (.02)	108 (.87)
Government	16 (.41)	23 (.59)	10 (.26)
Library	1 (.02)	2 (.04)	44 (.94)
Museum	0 (.00)	0 (.00)	1 (1.00)
Other	2 (.14)	10 (.14)	10 (.71)
Parks & Zoo	14 (.19)	25 (.25)	40 (.56)
Religious	0 (.00)	0 (.00)	26 (1.00)
Total	65 (.16)	69 (.17)	333 (.73)

than one site (See Table 8). The highest levels of duplication were noted for the events organized by the city government and the arts-related organizations (41 and 19 percent respectively).

Another indication of redundancy in the online event information landscape is the degree to which events found on the neighborhood sites are also found in the baseline information source (i.e., the community's newspaper of record). Overall, 17 percent of events found in the sampled sites were also found in the online version of *Post-Gazette*, either in its Events section or in news articles (See Table 8). The events duplicated in this fashion most frequently were also sponsored by city governments (59 percent). The parks and zoo, arts-related, and community organizations also had some duplication between the newspaper and other online event information sources (25, 18, and 15 percent respectively).

However, most events (73 percent) were listed on only one of the neighborhood sites and were not found in the *Post-Gazette*. Events collected from religious institutions were not found anywhere else. Most library events were exclusively advertised on the library web site (94 percent). A large share of the events organized by community organizations and entertainment organizations were also found in a single source (83 and 87 percent, respectively) (See Figure 5).

Online event information has a low level of duplication. A small proportion of events was found in the newspaper of record and a majority of events was found in only one of the sampled sites. While the level of overall duplication of

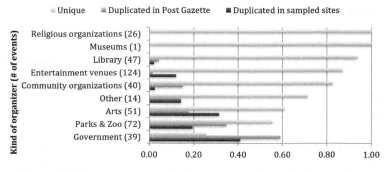

Figure 5: Uniqueness and duplication of event information by organizer.

event data was quite low, the proportion of duplicated events still varied significantly among organizer types.

How Fragmented is the Online Event Information Landscape?

Another potentially significant feature of online information landscapes is the degree of centralization/fragmentation. Preferential attachment in online networks is argued to lead to structures in which a small number of sites, sources, or individuals occupy highly central positions (Adamic and Huberman, 2000). In the studied neighborhoods there are suggestions of a similar structure with traditional media sites advertising a larger number of events than other types of sites (See Table 9). Together, the three traditional media sites and the *Post-Gazette* provided information about 38 percent of the events while social media only covered 13 percent. The parks and zoo and the entertainment sites also had information about a large proportion of events (25 and 23 percent); however, as noted above, these sites usually focused on providing information about their own events.

Closer examination of site-level results indicates that no single site accounted for a dominant share of the local events (See Table 9). The *Post-Gazette* covered the largest share of the identified local events (17 percent), a surprisingly small proportion given the newspaper's mission and its attempts to serve as a key source of local event information. Among the other sites, one of the entertainment organizations and the *Pittsburgh City Paper* (an "alternative newspaper") had information about 14 percent of the events. The rest of the sites covered even smaller proportions of the total of local events.

In contrast to what preferential attachment and critical mass arguments might suggest, no single site or type of site occupied a particularly "central" location in the local event information landscape (See Figure 6). Even sites that were nominally focused on providing information for the local community, such as traditional media and libraries, covered at most a small fraction of the events that were mentioned in online information sources. Online information about local events is highly fragmented.

Do Organizers' and Sites' Resource Models Affect Local Event Information?

Organizers with different missions and resource models (non-profit, for-profit, etc.) do not differ significantly in the number of events that they organize. Among the

Table 9: Fragmentation of the events information.

	# Events covered by this type of site	# Events covered by the top site of this type
Arts	5 (.01)	5 (.01)
Community	35 (.08)	19 (.05)
Entertainment	95 (.23)	57 (.14)
Government	49 (.12)	49 (.12)
Library	49 (.12)	49 (.12)
Parks & Zoo	104 (.25)	52 (.13)
Religious	20 (.05)	13 (.03)
Social media	52 (.13)	28 (.07)
Traditional media	157 (.38)	69 (.17)

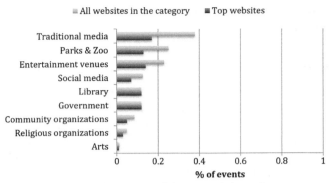

Figure 6: Fragmentation of the events information.

event organizers, 69 institutions were classified according their resource model (See Table 10). Twenty-nine for-profit institutions were responsible for 39 percent of the events and organized an average of 5.59 events each. Forty organizers are non-profits. They offered 45 percent of the events and they arranged 4.68 events on average. Six religious organizations arranged around four events on average. Four city government organizations offered more events than any of the other categories. However, these differences were not statistically significant ($p = .553$).

When the events were announced on other organizations' web sites (i.e., not the organizer's site), they mostly appeared on for-profit web sites. As a group, for-profit web sites had data about at least one event from 68 percent of the event organizers, while collectively non-profit web sites included information from only 22 percent of the organizers (See Table 11). City government web sites disseminated information from other city governments and from the non-profits, but none from for-profits. Religious sites did not advertise events from any other type of organization.

Table 10: Events by organizers' resource model.

Organizers' resources model	# Organizers	# Events	Mean	% of total
For-profit	29	162	5.59	.39
Non-profit	40	187	4.68	.45
Government	4	39	9.75	.09
Religious	6	26	4.33	.06

Table 11: Sites that advertise third-party events by resource model.

	Sites' resources model				
Organizers' resources model	For-profit	Non-profit	Government	Religious	Post Gazette
For-profit	28 (.97)	1 (.03)	0 (.00)	0 (.00)	6 (.21)
Non-profit	20 (.50)	15 (.38)	6 (.15)	0 (.00)	13 (.33)
Government	1 (.25)	2 (.50)	1 (.25)	0 (.00)	3 (.75)
Religious	5 (.83)	0 (.00)	0 (.00)	0 (.00)	0 (.00)
Total	54 (.68)	18 (.22)	7 (.08)	0 (.00)	22 (.27)

In general, sites also seemed to be biased towards events organized by organization with a similar resource model (See Figure 7). For-profits sites contained information about events run by almost all of the for-profit organizers, but they covered events from only half of the non-profits. Conversely, while non-profits' web sites had information from a much lower proportion of the event organizers, they were much more likely to publicize events from other non-profits (38 percent) than from for-profit organizations (3 percent).

Events that were organized by for-profit and non-profit organizations had lower rates of duplication than those sponsored by city government (See Table 12). For-profit organizations were marginally more likely than non-profits to have events duplicated among the neighborhood sites ($p = .053$). Unexpectedly, events from non-profits were more frequently available on the *Post-Gazette* than those offered by for-profit organizations. The higher levels of duplication of non-profits' events were influenced by the events organized by the zoo and large arts organizations, which were well promoted. On the other hand, some of the for-profit organizations were small entertainment promoters that organized many small-scale events that were not listed on other web sites. All religious events were found on single sites. Events supported by the government were less likely to be advertised on unique sites than those organized by others. However, non-profits and for-profit organizers were equally likely to advertise their events in a single site (i.e., not be duplicated).

Regarding fragmentation, for-profit sites accounted for the largest share of the total event count (73 percent), while non-profits' share was 47 percent (See Table 13). Furthermore, on average, for-profit sites had information about more events than non-profit web sites.

Together these results imply that while organizations with different resource models do not seem to differ significantly in their ability or tendency to run events,

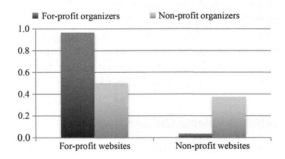

Figure 7: Proportion of sites announcing events of organizations.

Table 12: Duplication of event information by organizers' resource model.

Organizers' resources model	Duplicated in sampled sites	Duplicated in *Post Gazette*	Unique
For-profit	29 (.18)	8 (.05)	130 (.80)
Non-profit	20 (.11)	38 (.20)	137 (.73)
Government	16 (.41)	23 (.59)	23 (.26)
Religious	0 (.00)	0 (.00)	26 (1.00)

Table 13: Fragmentation by site resource model.

Sites' resources model	# Sites	# Events	Mean
For-profit	9	304 (.73)	33.8
Non-profit	7	193 (.47)	27.5
Government	1	49 (.12)	49.0
Religious	3	20 (.05)	6.7

they differ significantly in their ability to use the local event information infrastructure, with for-profit sites and organizers being better at gathering, and further promoting information about events.

Who Adds and Manages Local Event Information?

Sites within the local information landscape also differ with respect to how they gather and manage information about events. Fully moderated models are those in which only site administrators can add events. Partially moderated sites allow users to submit events, but an administrator decides whether it will be added to the site. User-enabled models allow any user to add events to the site. All thirteen of the sites run by event organizers used a fully moderated model. All of the six of the traditional media and social media sites used a user-based model. Three-hundred fifty seven out of 414 events were found in fully moderated sites. One hundred forty events were found in user-based sites (See Table 14).

Among the neighborhood sites, duplicated events were more common on user-enabled sites (43 percent) than moderated sites (22 percent). The opposite pattern (Fully-moderated > User-based) was found for duplication in the *Post-Gazette*. Events on user-enabled sites were significantly less likely to be unique than those found in fully moderated web sites (54 vs. 65 percent). Overall, this suggests that user-enabled models are more likely to gather information about local events that is available elsewhere online, reducing fragmentation of the local information space (See Figure 8). However, the total number of events accounted for by user-enabled sites is still limited.

Is the Event Information Available Online Complete?

A well-constructed event description provides information such as: title, description, date/time, and venue. If this data is missing, users will find it difficult to decide whether or not to attend an event. Overall, the neighborhood sites tended to provide complete information about events with only 10 percent of the events having incomplete information on the initial site where

Table 14: Duplication rates and moderation models.

Sites' resources model	# Sites	# Events	Duplicated in sampled sites	Duplicated in *Post Gazette*	Unique
Fully-moderated	13	357	78 (.22)	80 (.23)	233 (.65)
User-based	6	140	60 (.43)	20 (.14)	76 (.54)

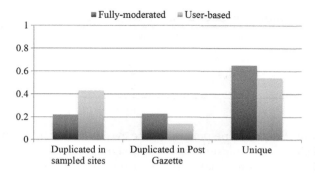

Figure 8: Uniqueness and duplication of event information by moderation style.

they were found. Sites that relied on users to provide event information were twice as likely to have incomplete information as fully moderated sites (16 vs. 8 percent) (See Figure 9). At the same time, these user-based sites were more likely to provide links to other sites where complete event data was available (60 vs. 39 percent). This shows that user-based systems are more likely than fully moderated systems to be acting as intermediaries that provide traces of events information that encourage users to look for additional information in other sources.

Do the Geographical Focuses of the Sites Matter?

In addition to their content gathering and management strategies, sites also differ with respect to their geographic scope. Of the neighborhood event information sites, 11 were focused on a single neighborhood, six targeted the whole city, and two were social sites with a national scope. Although they varied with respect to their overall focus, these sites did not differ significantly with respect to the average number of locally relevant events that they provided information about (See Table 15).

However, the geographic scope of the sites was significantly associated with the duplication and fragmentation of events information (See Figure 10). Sites focused on single neighborhoods had a higher proportion of unique information, thus contributing to the high degree of fragmentation in the local events infor-

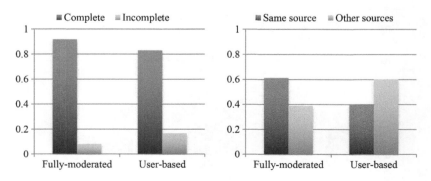

Figure 9: Complete information and links to other sources by moderation style.

Table 15: Sites by their geographical focus.

Sites' focus	# Sites	# Events	Mean	Std. dev.
Neighborhood	11	256 (.62)	23	21
City	6	190 (.46)	32	25
Country	2	52 (.13)	26	3

mation landscape. Sevent- nine percent of the events that were found in neighborhood-oriented sites were unique. This ratio is significantly larger than the percentages of duplication in sites that had a broader geographical scope (39 and 60 percent for city and country web sites, respectively). Furthermore, information that was found in sites with the narrowest scope (neighborhood) and with the broadest scope (country-level) was rarely found duplicated in the citywide media site (*Post-Gazette*).

As expected, the neighborhood-oriented sites had predominantly information about events happening in their corresponding neighborhoods. More than 76 percent of the events advertised in these web sites were located in their targeted neighborhood. The events that were advertised in a single source were generally small-scale concerts, parties/social events, and family/children events. These events were usually held in small-scale entertainment venues, library branches, and community organizations. On the other hand, arts-related events such as exhibitions in local art galleries tended to be posted in social media sites with national scope, but they were often not found in the city's newspaper of record.

Further exploration of the events' locations showed that our sampled neighborhoods varied in terms of the kinds of events that they hosted. A large majority of the events in Bloomfield were concerts happening in entertainment venues, and events happening in art galleries and theatres. Highland Park's events were highly influenced by the activities in the zoo and the park located in the neighborhood. East Liberty and Squirrel Hill had more diverse spectrums of events. Both neighborhoods had several events held in their library branches. East Liberty also had a considerable proportion of events in entertainment venues and religious organizations. On the other hand, Squirrel

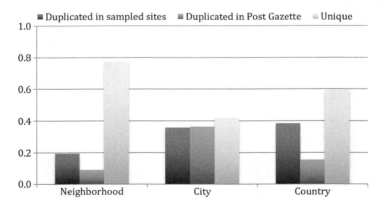

Figure 10: Duplication and uniqueness of data by web sites' geographical focus.

Hill also had a substantial number of events that were located in its parks and community organizations. Although the neighborhoods varied in their dominant types of events (and their venues), we did not find evidence that these four neighborhoods varied considerably in their total number of advertised events. Even though it could have been expected to find some significant variation on the number of advertised events across neighborhoods due to their diverse demographics and socioeconomic differences, our data did not provide support for that claim. It is possible that the limited sample size of four neighborhoods was not sufficient to detect these differences. Alternatively, it is also possible that the fact that our sampled neighborhoods were adjacent to one another might have confounded the relationship between neighborhood characteristics and the number of advertised events.

Discussion

Dissemination of event information is a necessary condition for keeping residents aware of what is going on in their community. While the emergence of widely available Web technologies over the past decade has created the possibility of online sources of information about local events, decision makers, developers, and researchers still must make many assumptions when working with communities' local event information infrastructures.

Our results indicate that while local event information can be found online, it is dispersed across many online sites each of which provides a small amount of local event data. There is a low rate of replication of local event information among sites and with traditional media sources (including the citywide newspaper of record) and no one organization covers a significant proportion of the total local event set. Together these results highlight the complex nature of the information seeking and information management problems presented by local events. Even in just four neighborhoods, the volume of events (400+) and frequency of events (four to five per day) is significant. While low levels of duplication may help minimize information overload, combined with the fragmented source landscape it places significant burdens on individuals seeking to keep up with events in their community. These results help to explain why Americans still do not rely on the Web as the main source of information about local events, instead continuing to depend on many different sources including word of mouth (Rosenstiel et al., 2011).

Our findings also show that the local events described in neighborhood sites differ considerably from the events posted in and by a highly visible citywide traditional media source (our baseline). While local information sources cover social events and small-scale concerts located in the neighborhoods, the primary traditional media source provides more information about charities, events for families and children, and large-scale concerts. Overall, the traditional media sources offered a very limited subset of the events covered in the aggregate of the other local sources, revealing that the overall number of events in these communities is much larger than what can be found in a single traditional media source. Considering the full range of other sites, including social media, increases the scope and diversity of the events that are announced online.

Although the Web allows for widespread dissemination and easy access to information, for local events this potential has not yet been realized. Fragmentation, dormant event sites, and incomplete data means that finding or tracking information about events that might be of interest is likely to require significant time and effort. Moderated, managed information sources provide higher quality data. But these sites often offer collections of events that reflect sponsoring organization priorities that may or may not coincide with community members' interests. User-generated event information has the potential to fill this gap, increasing the likelihood that the event information present in a community reflects the interest of the people who reside there. However, a critical obstacle is that the proportion of events found in user-based sites was quite limited compared to fully moderated sites. Nevertheless, some positive signs were still observed. First, the rate of duplicated events in user-based sites was almost twice larger than the rate of duplication in moderated sites. Second, user-based sites also tended to have a larger proportion of incomplete events information than fully moderated sites, and they provided more external links to get the complete information about events. This way, sites that rely on user-generated content confirm their role in increasing duplication, and hence visibility, of data in the information landscape and integrating information from sites that would not otherwise be easily accessible. A preliminary analysis of the external links that did not lead to our sampled sites showed that the duplication of data increases to 52 percent when considering the complete pool of 134 different sites referenced by the sampled sites. It is interesting to notice that this larger pool of event-related sites led us to other actors in the events information landscape, such as ticket sellers and Facebook. However, none of them reported on more than 6 percent of the sampled events, thus confirming the high level of fragmentation in local events information landscapes. Together these results indicate that while use of user-enabled platforms to collect and share local information broadly is technically possible and some nascent signs of their potential can be observed, at least in these communities, this has not yet successfully emerged as a dominant, comprehensive source of event information.

Another factor associated with the duplication of event information was the geographical scope of the event information sources. A majority of the studied sites focused on a single neighborhood. These neighborhood-oriented sites were much more likely to have unique information about local events, giving them a distinctive identity while increasing the overall fragmentation. A resident seeking to keep informed about events in their community would need to check many sites that each provide small amounts of unique information about events in order to develop an overall sense of what events are happening. On the other hand, large social sites with a national scope also contained information about events that were usually not found in the traditional local media sites. Overall, these findings hint at an emerging community information ecology in which locally-focused sources, regional media, and nationally (or even globally) scoped systems play complementary roles as sources for event information.

Although we collected data from a small number of sites associated with four neighborhoods, we gathered information from 79 event organizers. Traditional media and social media sites contained information about many types of events from many kinds of event organizers. Notably, community organizations, but not the city library, also played a role as disseminators of other organizers' events. Additionally, there was only one very active partnership among events organizers to advertise each other's events (the city government and the city parks organization). This shows that events organizers have generally continued using media to advertise their own information, but have not typically been either willing or able to expand their channels sites even when the technical cost of doing so is negligible.

Our results also showed that while non-profits and for-profits do not differ in the number of events that they organize, for-profit sites are able and willing to provide information about a greater share of events than non-profit sites. This could affect the long-term viability of the non-profits sites as sources of local event information because they might eventually fail to provide enough events and become inactive. At the same time, sites tended to advertise more events run by organizers with similar resource models. Non-profits web sites announced more events from other non-profits, and for-profits web sites advertised more events from other for-profits. Overall, this suggests that for-profits have been more successful at developing and mobilizing the online technologies to create a local event information infrastructure that meets their needs.

Limitations

As with any other research project, our study has limitations that should be taken into account when interpreting the findings and assessing its contributions. First, although the importance of event information is generally accepted as a key component of event management, it is still unknown what is the impact of information availability on event attendance, civic engagement, and other relevant impacts and outcomes. Our study provides an approach for assessing the characteristics of local information landscapes. Future work can address related research questions such as the impact of these characteristics in actual attendance of local events, individuals' perceptions of their communities, and community resilience. Second, we did not find significant differences on the number of advertised events across the four sampled neighborhoods. However, the small sample may not have had sufficient power to reveal true relationships between neighborhood characteristics and the features of the community's event information infrastructure. Alternatively, the close proximity of the four neighborhoods may have obscured the neighborhood level effects. Further research is needed to better assess the impact of communities and their demographics on the levels of dissemination of event information. Third, we conducted our data collection on neighborhoods in a US mid-sized city. Therefore, our findings may not apply to communities with substantially different characteristics such as rural communities, neighborhoods in other countries, or neighborhoods with considerably different demographics. Replicating this study in other communities can help to address this limitation and increase the generalizability of the conclusions. Fourth, our investigation focused on the distribution of event information on the Web only. Future research can consider how Web, mobile, and more traditional offline information systems combine to affect the generation, dissemination, and use of local event information.

Conclusion

While prior research has identified the positive impacts of local events on social capital and civic engagement, the understanding of how people learn about, get involved in, and share information about these community activities is still limited. Particularly, even though event data dissemination is recognized as a key factor in event management, it is still unclear how event information availability affects people's participation in local events. This study aims to begin addressing this gap by shedding light on the characteristics of the information infrastructure that underlies community residents' access to local event data.

This paper reports a fine-grained analysis of the online landscape of event information sources for four neighborhoods in a mid-sized US city. Our findings indicate that the main characteristics of this information infrastructure are:

- *Low duplication* of event information among online sources of local event data and with traditional media sources; more than 70 percent of the local events were found in a single online source.
- *High fragmentation* of event information across many online sites that offer small shares of the overall event data; no single site covered more than 20 percent of the entire set of local events.
- *Larger scope and higher diversity* of advertised local events is available through the complete range of online sources of event data, in aggregate, than is announced in the citywide newspaper of record.
- The *potential for widespread data dissemination through user-based sites has not yet been realized* in the distribution of local event information, but some positive signs were observed. User-based sites covered a limited share of the local events, which decreased its impact on the characteristics of the overall event information landscape. Nonetheless, these sites increased both duplication of event data and visibility of external sources that would not otherwise be accessible.

From an organizational perspective, we also identified the following characteristics of the event information ecosystem:

- It brings together *organizations with different missions, resource models, and geographical reach*. Through different mechanisms, these organizations play complementary roles as event organizers and event information sources/disseminators.
- Although non-profit and for-profit event organizers do not differ in their capacity to run events, for-profit sites and organizers are more effective than non-profit ones at gathering and further disseminating data about local events.

Future work should consider technical, managerial, and policy interventions that might be undertaken to strengthen non-profit organizations' ability to develop and leverage the infrastructure they need to successfully run high-impact local event sites.

Overall these findings suggest that efforts to consolidate, organize, and leverage local event information face a challenging infrastructure design problem. Relying on the dominant, traditional media sources is likely to provide only limited coverage of the full range and diversity of local events. Integrating information from multiple sources might be used to overcome this limitation. However, successful integration would require identification and monitoring of many small, often ephemeral sites associated with significantly different types of organizations. Yet, failing to identify these types of sites would significantly reduce the coverage to a data collection effort. Another common strategy involves partnering with particular organizations. However, the degree of fragmentation and the diversity of site types and event organizers are likely to make creating and maintaining the necessary partnerships complex and labor intensive.

While our findings provide a useful start for better understanding how we collectively gather, disseminate, and manage local event information, additional work is needed to characterize the challenges, solutions, and opportunities associated with this critical, but often overlooked aspect of modern urban communities. Further research can build on this work by exploring how the characteristics of event information landscapes (e.g., duplication, fragmentation) affect residents' awareness about local events, participation in them, and residents' civic engagement and social capital.

Notes

1. <http://metromix.com> Accessed October 23, 2014.
2. <http://eventful.com/> Accessed October 23, 2014.
3. <http://www.post-gazette.com/> Accessed October 23, 2014.
4. This table only includes event types that accounted for more than 0.001 percent of the events.
5. These neighborhoods were defined based on City of Pittsburgh documents. While assessing accuracy of these boundaries is beyond the scope of this study, these designations are generally consistent with those used by residents and local media.
6. The number of events in each neighborhood varies from −1 to +2 standard deviations around average number of events in the baseline dataset
7. Preliminary examination of the first 40 search results showed that after the twentieth result there were almost no event-related pages.
8. Three of them categorized as "Web info provider" and the other one classified as "Other."

Bibliography

L.A. Adamic and B.A. Huberman, "Power-Law Distribution of the World Wide Web," *Science* 287 (2000) 2115–2115.

C. Arcodia and M. Whitford, "Festival Attendance and the Development of Social Capital," *Journal of Convention & Event Tourism* 8 (2006) 1–18.

A. Brajsa-Zganec, M. Merkas, and I. Sverko, "Quality of Life and Leisure Activities: How do Leisure Activities Contribute to Subjective Well-Being?," *Social Indicators Research* 102 (2011) 81–91.

M.J. Daniels and W.C. Norman, "Estimating the Economic Impacts of Seven Regular Sport Tourism Events," *Journal of Sport & Tourism* 8 (2003) 214–222.

T.A. Delamere, L.M. Wankel, and T.D. Hinch, "Development of a Scale to Measure Resident Attitudes Toward the Social Impacts of Community Festivals, Part I: Item Generation and Purification of the Measure," *Event Management* 7 (2001) 11–24.

R. Derrett, "Festivals and Regional Destinations: How Festivals Demonstrate a Sense of Community & Place," *Rural Society* 13 (2003) 35–53.

D. Getz, "The Nature and Scope of Festival Studies," *International Journal of Event Management Research* 5 (2010) 1–47.

D. Getz and W. Frisby, "Developing a Municipal Policy for Festivals and Special Events," *Recreation Canada* 49 (1991) 42–44.

R. Giesecke, *The Event Management Ecosystem*, Aalto University, School of Science (2011).

W.J. Goudy, "Evaluations of Local Attributes and Community Satisfaction in Small Towns," *Rural Sociology* 42:3 (1977) 371–382.

D. Gursoy, K. Kim, and M. Uysal, "Perceived Impacts of Festivals and Special Events by Organizers: An Extension and Validation," *Tourism Management* 25 (2004) 171–181.

M. Gurstein, ed., *Enabling Communities with Information and Communications Technologies*, (New York: IGI Global, 1999).

Kantar-Media, "UK Demand for Hyperlocal Media," Nesta (2013). <http://www.nesta.org.uk/sites/default/files/uk_demand_for_hyperlocal_media.pdf> Accessed October 23, 2014

T. Kay and S. Bradbury, "Youth Sport Volunteering: Developing Social Capital?," *Sport, Education and Society* 14 (2009) 121–140.

K.-H. Lee and D.-Y. Kim, "The Influence of Geographical Distance Groups (GDGs) on Visitor's Information Sources and Motivations in Local Festival Settings," (International CHRIE Conference-Refereed Track. 2011).

K. Lloyd and C. Auld, "The Role of Leisure in Determining Quality of Life: Issues of Content and Measurement," *Social Indicators Research* 57 (2002) 43–71.

C.A. López and B.S. Butler, "Consequences of Content Diversity for Online Public Spaces for Local Communities," *Proc. CSCW* (2013) 673–682.

T.L. Mayfield and J.L. Crompton, "Development of an Instrument for Identifying Community Reasons for Staging a Festival," *Journal of Travel Research* 33 (1995) 37–44.

L. Misener and D.S. Mason, "Creating Community Networks: Can Sporting Events Offer Meaningful Sources of Social Capital?," *Managing Leisure* 11 (2006) 39–56.

N. Ntloko and K. Swart, "Sport Tourism Event Impacts on the Host Community—A Case Study of Red Bull Big Wave Africa," *South African Journal for Research in Sport, Physical Education and Recreation* 30 (2008) 79–93.

R.D. Putman, Bowling Alone: The Collapse and Revival of American Community (New York: Simon & Schuster, 2000).

T. Rosenstiel, A. Mitchell, K. Purcell, and L. Rainie, *How People Learn About Their Local Community* (Washington, DC: Pew Research Center, 2011).

P. Sherwood, "A Triple Bottom Line Evaluation of the Impact of Special Events: The Development of Indicators," (Victoria University, 2007).

K.A. Smith, "Distribution Channels for Events: Supply and Demand-side Perspectives," *Journal of Vacation Marketing* 13 (2007) 321–338.

K.A. Smith, "The Information Mix for Events: A Comparison of Multiple Channels Used by Event Organisers and Visitors," *International Journal of Event Management Research* 4 (2008) 24–37.

G.L. Theodori, "Examining the Effects of Community Satisfaction and Attachment on Individual Well-Being*," *Rural Sociology* 66 (2001) 618–628.

G. Waitt, "The Olympic Spirit and Civic Boosterism: The Sydney 2000 Olympics," *Tourism Geographies* 3 (2001) 249–278.

B. Wellman, "Physical Place and Cyberplace: The Rise of Personalized Networking," *International Journal of Urban and Regional Research* 25 (2001) 227–252.

L. Wilks, "Bridging and Bonding: Social Capital at Music Festivals," *Journal of Policy Research in Tourism, Leisure and Events* 3 (2011) 281–297.

Appendix

Table 16: Examples of event coding.

Event	Sampled web site	Organizer	Venue's neighborhood	Type of event
24 Hours in the Subway: Pastel by Isabelle Garbani	Pittsburgh city paper	Box Heart Gallery	Bloomfield	Exhibits / Visual arts
CLP-East Liberty: Happy Anniversary!	Carnegie Library, East Liberty	Carnegie Library, East Liberty	East Liberty	Parties / Socials
Reservoir of Jazz	Pittsburgh Council	Highland Park	Highland Park	Music concert
Blackbird Pie	Metromix	Grey Box Theatre	Lawrenceville	Theater / Performing arts

Goals, Challenges, and Capacity of Regional Data Portals in the United States: An Updated Understanding of Long-Standing Discussions

Joanna P. Ganning, Sarah L. Coffin, Benjamin McCall, and Kathleen Carson

ABSTRACT *Online participation in political processes has grown in advanced industrial societies like the United States (E. Anduiza, A. Gallego, and M. Cantijoch, "Online Political Participation in Spain: The Impact of Traditional and Internet Resources," Journal of Information Technology & Politics 7: 4 (2010) 356–368). Experimentation and goal-setting have been done around integrating two-way communication into online GIS portals to advance online participation. Increasingly, web development information technology enables the development of these functions. However, the state of practice has not developed to support such activities. This paper relies on literature and a survey of US geoportals to provide an in-depth overview of the state of practice for such sites, including stated goals and challenges, current applications, and both technical and realized capabilities. This paper then discusses this state of practice through the lens of the development process of a new geoportal for the St Louis region. This discussion yields a response to issues raised in the literature and provides a framework for other groups that are considering development of similar sites.*

Introduction

In many cities across the United States, metropolitan and regional data portals provide web-based GIS and data services to citizens, university researchers, non-profits, and government agencies. These portals often provide tabular data, spatial data, and in some cases, static maps and research reports. These portals usually provide access to these services free of charge to registered users, asking only for proper source citation when contents are used in applications or reports. In recent years the open source web development community has enabled drastic improvements in the functionality, design, and user experience of these sites. Despite these advancements, and as we discuss in detail below, the ability of such sites to meet the needs of planning and public administration processes remains in question.

This paper aims to provide academics and practitioners with a full overview of the state of regional data portals, with a discussion of lessons learned from implementing one case study project. This overview is presented to help guide planning agencies, universities, regional governments, and municipalities in the conceptual framing of similar, new sites. This overview comes in three parts: (1) background on the case study and related terminology; (2) the state of practice and web development capability (providing an overview of the applications, stated goals of data portals, stated challenges, state of practice, and state of technical capability); and (3) discussion synthesizing the prior two sections into an examination of approaches to pragmatic data portal development processes. Insights gleaned from the case study project are woven throughout, to contextualize themes found in the literature and provide detail.

Somewhat surprisingly, we find that two warnings issued long ago in the literature on computer-aided planning still apply, though with added nuances that the authors could not have anticipated at the time. The first of these two warnings cautions that "the most important obstacles to computer-aided planning will not be solved by technological advances alone, for even the most ambitious of the early development models rarely exceeded the computational limits of the mainframe computers of the era" (Klosterman, 1987: 443). Second, we must agree with Drummond and French (2008), who concluded that planners interested in leveraging online GIS for public participation in planning processes must continue to engage with the web development community to ensure that adequate tools are being programmed. The technical capacity to build fully electronic public participation GIS (PPGIS)-based online data portals has evolved, but issues of participation, bias, and producing tools for specific applications that remain user-friendly continue to plague the development of such sites.

Background

This section first reviews relevant terminology, which frames the remainder of the paper. Following those definitions, this section provides an overview of the case study website, the St Louis Regional Data Exchange.

Terminology

The introduction of this paper discusses data portals that provide public participation advantages centered on GIS technology. What is PPGIS? "PPGIS refers to the use of GIS technology to support and empower public participation in planning, natural resource management, and policy development (Sieber, 2006)" (Pocewicz et al., 2012: 40). Beyond that, however, the definition becomes inconsistent, depending largely on the social context of use. While PPGIS does not necessarily have to be a data portal—it could entail GIS technology on tablet devices or even paper maps for use in surveys—a data portal, as defined below, clearly fits within the definition of PPGIS.

The St Louis Regional Data Exchange meets the definition of a "geoportal." The site uses Spatial Data Infrastructure (SDI) to "connect distributed repositories of geospatial information (GI) and make these available to users through a single entry point" (Budhathoki et al., 2008: 149). Alternately,

> a geo-portal is a web-based system that allows users to discover particular geo-datasets by looking into the associated metadata, to portray the data

on a map, and to retrieve the data in adequate formats to further process them in a professional workflow. (Resch and Zimmer, 2013: 1019)

These sites have not traditionally integrated Volunteered Geographic Information (VGI), though VGI sites attract millions of users across the world (e.g., openstreetmap.org). As Bugs et al. (2010: 173) describe: "In general, users can post comments on a map, but user-friendly, map-based citizen's opinion and interactive discussion is still not widely supported." Though technological constraints to creating such sites are gradually diminishing, Bugs et al. (2010) remain correct that VGI is not being frequently incorporated into geoportals (herein data portals), as the survey of sites presented below shows.

Case Study

A Sustainable Communities Regional Planning grant received by the East-West Gateway Council of Governments and funded by the Department of Housing and Urban Development's Office of Sustainable Housing and Communities[1] enabled the development of a new data portal for the region. The data portal was created by the Applied Research Collaborative (ARC), a long-standing, informal research consortium of applied policy researchers at Saint Louis University's Center for Sustainability, University of Missouri-St Louis' Public Policy Research Center, and the Institute for Urban Research at Southern Illinois University at Edwardsville. The three-year data portal development process involved assembling a committee of stakeholders and contracting with a web developer, reviewing the state of the art of regional data portals, going through a visioning process for the web portal and ultimately developing the site,[2] the St Louis Regional Data Exchange. This process began in 2011.

This site was designed to offer both pre-made static maps and user-generated maps assembled from spatial data contributed to the site by portal members. Membership is open to the public, with an approval process for becoming a "data provider," to those users who can contribute data sets. Users can comment on maps that other users either upload as static maps or generate and save through the portal. A potential second stage for the portal would involve integration with social media, ideally allowing users to contribute VGI such as geotagged photographs or attribute information about places. In the first stage, however, the goals were to enable data sharing, provide GIS services for planners and other professionals requiring maps for grant applications and similar products, and to provide a database for regional planning efforts. Notably, East-West Gateway originally hoped the portal would allow community members to set parameters for regional scenario planning and see the implications of those scenarios modeled, relying on underlying modeling that would run in the background. While this was beyond reach for the portal, the portal does provide a link to the larger project site, OneSTL (http://www.onestl.org/). Efforts to host content for the larger project's Environmental Best Practices Toolkit also proved technically challenging as the larger project's goals shifted. At present, the online toolkit found on the OneSTL site provides links to the data portal but does not draw data directly from the portal. The data portal officially launched in the spring of 2013. As of March 2014 there were 170 unique users who had collectively contributed 116 GIS data sets and produced 18 interactive maps.

The State of Practice for PPGIS-Based Data Portals

This section provides a discussion of applications for PPGIS, and an overview of the stated goals and challenges for such sites as provided by the literature. This section also provides the results of a survey of data portals conducted in February 2014, summarizing the functionality of 37 websites. These sources are then synthesized in the discussion section to provide a view, rooted in practice and academic research, of a pragmatic approach to data portal projects for agencies and municipalities.

Applications

A review of literature reveals that PPGIS is being used across the globe, and for a range of uses. The evolution of computer-based methods in planning and public administration spans only a few decades. In an early publication on this topic, Klosterman (1987) describes the burgeoning promise of "micro computing" for economic models and planning intelligence. The industry changed dramatically over the following decade, seeing personal computers appear in homes and increasingly in the workplace, with an increasing cadre of functionalities. By century's end, Krygier (1999: 67) concluded that "In sum, the interactive mapping and GIS site designed as a prototype reveals that WWW-based mapping is certainly possible given adequate resources." As these texts reveal, prior to the twenty-first century, computer-based mapping was not accessible widely even to an academic audience, much less a lay audience.

The advent of PPGIS occurred somewhere between 1998 and 2000 through the incorporation of paper maps into survey instruments to gather place-based data (Brown, 2012). Over the course of the following decade (2000–2010), PPGIS methods evolved into fully-electronic platforms and paper/electronic hybrid survey instruments. These various forms of PPGIS were used to: measure changes in place values (Brown and Donovan, 2014); identify ecosystem services (Brown et al., 2012); improve landscape planning processes (Berry et al., 2011); collect visitor perspectives on natural and cultural resources for national park planning (Brown and Weber, 2011); define places (Brown and Weber, 2012); achieve immersive public participation in planning (Gordon et al., 2011); spatially represent place through qualitative methodological plurality (Lowery and Morse, 2013); and alert residents to disasters (Wang, 2012). Other papers tested whether paper-based or electronic PPGIS produced a higher participation rate (Brown, 2012; Pocewicz et al., 2012) and whether electronic PPGIS introduces a sampling bias (Brown et al., 2012; Brown et al., 2013). Additionally, a smaller literature (e.g., Harrie et al., 2011; Resch and Zimmer, 2013) discusses technical advancements in the field and efforts to standardize data portals (particularly in Europe), though much of this work has been confined to web development forums.

Stated Goals

PPGIS-based data portals often work toward multiple goals that are similar across applications, including increasing public participation rates, improving methods for gathering place-based data, and developing topic-specific applications such as disaster response tools. Based on a meta-analysis of 15 PPGIS studies, Brown

(2012: 7) concludes "that PPGIS has not substantively increased the level of public impact in decision making because of multiple social and institutional constraints ... agencies must meaningfully encourage and involve the public in planning processes irrespective of the GIS component." Other research shows that electronic PPGIS introduces bias into public participation samples (Brown et al., 2012; Brown et al., 2013). Due to these shortcomings in using computer-based PPGIS as survey instruments, these papers often conclude that a combination of paper- and computer-based PPGIS works, or that PPGIS provides a nice tool for supplementing expert opinion (on the latter, see Brown et al., 2012).

In addition to those goals, the literature indicates other goals that relate to broader planning applications for data portals, as opposed to the survey-based goals given above. A few studies present tests of paper- and computer-based map-centered public participation, implemented with the goal of devising two-way communication for planning via charrettes and scenario planning (Drummond and French, 2008; Rinner et al., 2008; Seeger, 2008). The efforts of the St Louis data portal around sustainability planning aptly highlight the challenges faced in using data portals and PPGIS for two-way planning communication. First, regional scenario planning relies on experts to define, collect, and create underlying metrics. Second, sophisticated spatial analysis tools and a large amount of computing capacity are required to model scenarios. For these reasons, simulations are being computed offline by experts with specialized software. While the model output is being made available for visualization on the portal, standard users cannot propose or model their own scenarios online. Beyond these issues, our group struggled to understand what data should be targeted for development and presentation on the portal. The region's definition of sustainability and chosen metrics for evaluation will have direct implications for the work that data providers do in order to participate in decision-making around issues of sustainability. That conversation requires elaborate collaboration among regional players which we found challenging, particularly in the early stages of the project. As in St Louis, data democratization has long been another goal, requisite with the challenges given in the following sub-section (Curtin, 2010).

Stated Challenges

A review of the literature found a number of potential challenges. By and large, the potential challenges for data portals are surmountable, though some require more effort than others, notably the legal issues related to data ownership. This sub-section presents the challenges as given in the literature, and presents the solution struck upon in the St Louis case study. This section does not review the proposed methods for addressing low participation rates in electronic PPGIS-based surveys, nor the issue of bias introduced in such surveys, as that discussion falls beyond the scope of this paper.

For a site like the portal, which does not involve significant VGI, three potential challenges raised independently in the literature can be grouped together: evaluating the validity and credibility of data (Elwood, 2008b), gatekeeping and authenticating data, and gauging whether professionals will accept data as valid (Flanagin and Metzger, 2008). Concerns over data validity and credibility have largely been mitigated by effective gatekeeping, thus persuading professionals to buy into the portal. Our gatekeeping process is simple: submit a request to site administrators to become a "data provider." Site administrators evaluate requests based on whether the person is a known data user in the region, what organization they are affiliated with, and whether they have provided faulty data in the past. Additionally, the portal was designed with functionality for users to red flag maps or data that are incorrect or otherwise inappropriate. These red flags allow site administrators to identify potential problem users (data providers or otherwise) and either follow up with them or rescind membership privileges.

However, gatekeeping does not mean that data are expected to be consistent across all metrics and data providers. Should the portal allow increased VGI in the future, we argue that the site's aim of improving regional planning also invites contradictions in data, which are not inherently negative; as Elwood (2008b: 179) argues, "contradictions in volunteered information may well be indications of social and political difference." She urges planners to "consider models of democratic practice that are effective in the face of uncertainty, contradiction, and diversity in spatial knowledge and spatial data" (2008b: 181).

Elwood (2008a) raises the issue of users offering data for which they have no right or permission to disseminate. The time-consuming search for solutions ultimately led us to a multi-pronged approach. First, early in the portal design process ARC approached the counties represented by the East-West Gateway Council of Governments to discuss including their GIS data on the portal. Those conversations yielded a list of geographies for which certain types of files were not allowable, permitting site administrators to immediately bar entry should a rogue data provider attempt upload. Second, the approval process for becoming a data provider was established in part to avoid such inappropriate contributions. Third, hosting the portal at a large university grants us access to legal guidance through the university. That legal counsel drafted language advising data providers to upload data at their own risk. Essentially this meant that parties who provided data were advised that the university hosting the data portal would not be reviewing legal claims to the data prior to publication. Should an outside party make a claim that inappropriate data were published on the portal, the university would remove it and advise the parties involved that they needed to settle the dispute before the data could be re-submitted. This terms-and-conditions approach to data publication provided much needed data liability relief for ARC and the East-West Gateway Council of Governments.

As a related issue, Elwood (2008b) raises the concern of data legality and validity in the context of data patchworking (Goodchild, 2007), a process in which local site users provide data that governments cannot or do not provide to the public. Working as a patchwork provider of data may work to our advantage. Where jurisdictions allocate resources toward maintaining sites with limited functionality and aging interfaces, there may be willingness to redirect that support to sites like the portal, which replace the older sites. That redirected support would help to alleviate concerns about portal maintenance, by allowing the university to employ students (who then gain experience) to respond to user requests, questions, and data flags. Additionally, while Flanagin and Metzger (2008) argue that sources like government agencies help to maintain the perceived credibility of data, we argue instead that a patchwork approach to public data provision improves on the eroded trust in those traditional sources. This may be especially true in shrinking cities such as St Louis were public budgets are stretched very thin. Inconsistent or poor record keeping by local governments in shrinking cities has been widely reported (e.g., Pagano and Bowman, 2000; Thomas, 2013). The patchwork approach helps to "free the data," though in a different method than that envisioned by Curtin (2010).

Budhathoki et al. (2008) and Klosterman (2008) raise the concern that SDI sites see low participation, which may relate to a need to evaluate the softer elements of facilitating computer-mediated planning (see Rhoads, 2010). In St Louis, "lunch & learn" training sessions were provided to mitigate this concern, though after one year, the usage statistics reported (170 unique users), remain lower than hoped. As mentioned in the introduction, we must agree with the historic literature that warned of the need to seek success beyond the technical capabilities of the sites (Klosterman, 1987).

Survey of Data Portals

Before starting the visioning process for the St Louis Regional Data Exchange, our research group surveyed the relevant literature and a national sample of 37 similar websites (See Appendix, Table A1). That work yielded an overview of functionalities and data sources, and allowed the group to identify the sites with the widest appeal for our regional audience and needs. Additionally, we reviewed the state of the underlying web programming that enables these sites. A review of that literature follows the portal survey results.

The sample of data portals varied in the functionalities offered (See Table 1, showing results updated to 2014). Some sites, such as Camden's CAMConnect, offer services limited to viewing pre-made maps, and require a fee-based registration. Sites such as the Des Moines Child and Family Policy Center have limited functionality catering to a specific audience. Other sites like the Minneapolis and Providence portals offer a wide array of features. As a group, the range of functionalities includes: prepared maps (19), data download (18), indicators (17), customized maps (10), query functionalities (9), application programming interface (API) access (6), the ability to e-mail or export maps (3), and customized charts and tables (1). Thirty of the sites offered public access, while six had restricted access. One site was under construction during the study period and one site was hacked.

Beyond functionality, portals surveyed showed tremendous variation in the roster of underlying data sources (See Table 1). Most sites display publicly available data like Census data (24). Many go beyond this, including employment (15) and employment projections (9), land use (5), transportation (5), natural resources information (2), orthophotographs and topographic quadrangles (2), and local media links (1). Here again, the sites range from providing little data to providing nearly all of the data listed here. The Minneapolis-St Paul Metropolitan Council's portal draws on an impressively wide range of data sources, providing data ranging from employment and housing to green infrastructure and land use.

As stated, the St Louis Regional Data Exchange was envisioned as an outlet where community members could upload, visualize, comment on, and download data. As such, its functionality (though perhaps not its range of data sources) is cutting-edge given the state of the art of data portals as shown in Table 1. Both the St Louis geoportal and Table 1 also show that overwhelmingly the distinction between SDI and VGI as described by Budhathoki et al. (2008; see also Elwood,

Table 1: Survey of data portals in the United States.

Data	# Sites
API	5
Type/Source of Information	
US Census (demographics)	20
US Census et al (spatial)	7
Bureau of Labor Statistics	2
STAT USA	1
US Bureau of Economic Analysis	1
Center for Disease Control	1
Population Projections	9
Employment	14
Employment Projections	8
Municipal (wages, land use, etc.)	7
Housing (foreclosures, etc.)	8
Safety (crime, etc.)	5
Education (test scores, etc.)	5
Imagery (USGS et al—includes the two below)	10
Orthophotographs	2
Topographic Quadrangles	2
Housing	18
Econometric (Geoda Center, National Longitudinal Surveys, Panel Study of Income Dynamics, etc.)	2
Health	3
Local Media (newspaper, etc.)	1
Watershed	2
Green Infrastructure	1
Land Use	5
Transportation	7
Natural Resources	3
Poverty	4
Indicators	17
Other	6
Functionality	
Download	18
Mapping	7
Generate Maps	12
Prebuilt Maps	19
Customize Map	10
Save Session/Map	3
Query	9
E-Mail	20
Customized reports	1
Security	
Public	28
Restricted (requires login but still free of charge)	6
Other	
Disclaimer	2

2008b) remains: data is being contributed overwhelmingly by expert users and members of authoritative sources such as city and county governments, councils of government, and universities. Additionally, these sites are generally not being used for the type of two-way communication for planning activities as has been envisioned (Drummond and French, 2008) or being tested using varying levels of sophistication (Rinner et al., 2008; Seeger, 2008; Bugs et al., 2010; see also Mandarano et al., 2010: 130). In part, this is because the technical capacity to support such activities has only recently evolved, or because the processing power required to support such services disallows on-the-fly feedback, as discussed in the case of regional scenario planning in St Louis.

Survey of Technical Capability in Web Development for Data Portals

In many regards, the St Louis portal represents the cutting edge not only of practice but also of technical capability. A growing number of GIS servers and web applications are capable of cataloging geographic data; however, a limited number of open-source applications meet the producer-focused SDI features envisioned by ARC for the St Louis Regional Data Exchange. Several active open-source geoportal software projects include: CKAN (ckan.org), Open Data Catalogue (github.com/azavea/Open-Data-Catalog), Geoportal Server (esri.com/software/arcgis/geoportal), and GeoNode (geonode.org). Each application differs in focus and features, has specific strengths and weaknesses, and is supported by distinct open-source development communities.

CKAN, from the Open Knowledge Foundation, is a popular and well-supported open-source data portal for documents and tabular data. A software plugin, the spatial data extension, adds geographic data set handling capabilities to CKAN. Producers can upload or provide links to data sets to a CKAN-powered geoportal and add descriptive metadata to their resources. Website visitors, or data consumers, can preview non-spatial data sets in table or chart format and geographic data in a simple, interactive map format. Consumers are able to provide feedback on data resources through comment forms and plugins, and producers have access to a robust API for enabling connections between CKAN and other applications or web services.

Similarly, the Open Data Catalogue (ODC) by Azavea allows producers to upload or link to spatial and non-spatial data sets for publishing on the geoportal. The ODC also allows producers to share links to online data APIs and data applications on third-party websites. Data consumers can search through the site's resources, view metadata, download or connect to data sources, and provide feedback through ratings and comments.

GeoPortal Server by ESRI allows producers to publish metadata and location information for their geographic resources. Unlike CKAN and ODC, which both catalog and store data sets, GeoPortal Server focuses solely on cataloging resources stored elsewhere. GeoPortal Server's website interface allows data consumers to search for and browse geographic data and web services, view a resource's metadata (which may include location and point of contact information), and connect to resources that are available from a publicly accessible GIS or web server. GeoPortal Server offers tight integration with other ESRI products, including ArcMap for Server.

The open-source geoportal selected by ARC is named GeoNode. This open-source application is supported by several organizations, including OpenGeo and the World Bank, as well as an active community of developers from around the world. GeoNode allows producers to upload and publish geographic data sets for sharing and discovery. The GeoNode documents extension also allows producers to upload and publish pre-made static maps. Like other geoportal applications, GeoNode allows consumers to preview spatial data in interactive map form, view each data set's metadata, and add comments and ratings to published resources. In addition, GeoNode's unique map composer feature allows data consumers to combine multiple data sets in a single map, customize layer styles, save the map for future reference, and optionally share the map with others. The map composer also allows authorized users to create, edit, or delete features on existing data sets. These added interactive mapping features transform traditional SDI users from data consumers into map producers, distinguish GeoNode from other geoportals, and were key factors in the software's selection to power the St Louis portal.

Discussion and Conclusion

This paper has framed the current state of data portals by stated goals, stated challenges, the state of practice, and the state of technical capabilities. Three general conclusions emerge from this framing. First, from the literature review, PPGIS (and perhaps data portals based on PPGIS) can be additive in qualitative research methods such as surveying, but only when special attention is paid to sampling size and bias, possibly via use of both paper- and computer-based methods. Second, intersecting the literature and our case study, the majority of concerns raised in the literature regarding portal construction and maintenance (data validity, legal issues, conflicting data, etc.) can be overcome in practice relatively easily. For each issue, a solution was found through our collaborative development process. Third, from the review of practice, the planning goals for PPGIS-based data portals, namely two-way communication in decision-making activities, such as charrettes and scenario planning, remain difficult to implement despite significant technical advancements.

A guiding question for VGI analysis applies to the current analysis of data portal and SDI effectiveness: "research needs to address the social, educational, and political outcomes ... by asking whether VGI assists, enables, or empowers, citizens and citizen organizations" (Flanagin and Metzger, 2008: 146). The answer to this question is complex. Certainly the St Louis Regional Data Exchange is valuable to regional researchers and planning practitioners. As stated in the Background section, the St Louis site (as of March 2014) has 170 unique registered users. Of those 170, 32 users registered an e-mail address with an education domain (.edu), and another six are university-affiliated but chose to use a personal e-mail address. Of the remaining 138 users, 43 registered e-mail addresses that stem from regional civic or planning organizations, such as East-West Gateway or the regional chamber of commerce. The remaining users have registered personal e-mail addresses with domains such as hotmail.com or gmail.com, or international addresses, particularly from Russia (nine users); the institutional memberships of these individuals cannot be ascertained. However, of the 170 unique registered users, nearly half are university affiliated or affiliated with civic or professional planning organizations. Given this professional focus of the data portal's membership and the three conclusions presented, two points from the literature bear further discussion and research.

First, Drummond and French (2008) raised a number of concerns regarding planning and GIS, which have been debated (Ferreira, 2008; Klosterman, 2008). From those, one concern has been borne out: planning, and cities more broadly, must continue to engage web developers to move toward the vision of two-way communication for online GIS-related applications. This is necessary for the critical, participatory, and feminist justifications for data democratization (Elwood, 2008b) and because political participation via online tools has become "increasingly relevant in advanced industrial societies" (Anduiza et al., 2010; Mandarano et al., 2010). As Gordon, Schirra, and Hollander (2011: 513) write:

> Many PPGIS function more like geographic sandboxes than tools for addressing specific problems, leaving it to the user to define his or her own parameters. So while this open-endedness seems pragmatic, allowing a single tool to serve endless spatial functions, its lack of specificity in some cases also means that users are left directionless and unengaged.

If researchers and practitioners want PPGIS-based data portals to do more than warehouse data and provide maps for reports, the functionality must be specific and tailored to those needs. As these needs (for instance, two-way communication for charrettes and scenario planning) are specific to planning, public administration, and perhaps engineering, it is those researchers who need to engage the web development community to produce the needed tools.

Second, the words of Klosterman (1987: 443) still ring true: "The first lesson to be learned is that the most important obstacles to computer-aided planning will not be solved by technological advances alone." Klosterman is correct in multiple regards. First, PPGIS-focused data portals like the one in St Louis would not work at all without regional planning processes that brought together the committee that developed the portal, held instructional seminars, and actively recruited data from regional stakeholders. Second, a regional data portal faces different challenges across communities. For instance, some declining cities have infamously poor data management skills (Pagano and Bowman, 2000; Thomas, 2013), predicating the value of data-sharing infrastructure on preceding steps toward data organization and improvement. Third, and perhaps most important, most regional data portals face long-term challenges in member recruitment and participation. As Brown (2012: 16) writes: "With greater saturation of Internet mapping applications, the novelty and potential attractiveness of participating in an Internet-based PPGIS may decline." Given the popularity of sites like Instagram, Twitter, and Facebook, the use of PPGIS-based data portals to gather citizen knowledge about places may seem to young citizens as geriatric as the "Every Third Wednesday at City Hall" format of zoning commission meetings.

In closing, one can synthesize this discussion into one overarching recommendation for cities and researchers engaging in the development of new PPGIS-based data portals: carefully consider goals. Doing so will maximize the productivity of time spent with web developers, and, if VGI is a goal, can identify the importance of and approach to branding and marketing the venture to the target audience. Goal-setting permeates every aspect of geoportal development, from addressing the challenges presented here, to meeting or exceeding the standard of practice, to choosing the appropriate web development approach for a site's stated goals. Our aim here has been to present a synthesized discussion of the uses, goals, challenges, state of practice, and technical capabilities, as perceived through the lens of a case study, in the hopes of providing scaffolding to other groups aiming to develop similar technical infrastructure within their communities.

Funding

This work was supported by the Department of Housing and Urban Development [MORIP0025-10].

Notes

1. Please note that the Office of Sustainable Housing and Communities is now the Office of Economic Resilience. For more information about the office and details regarding the federal program please see <http://portal.hud.gov/hudportal/HUD?src=/program_offices/economic_resilience>.
2. While the physical data portal described here came into existence only two years ago, work on a regional data system and regional data sharing began several years earlier, leading to the formation of ARC. In early 2005, Saint Louis University sponsored a data conference to discuss the state of data systems and practices in the region. The National Neighborhood Indicators Partnership (see <http://www.neighborhoodindicators.org/>) provided additional support, bringing speakers in from around the country who offered expertise on the state of the art in data democratization and community based regional data information systems.

Bibliography

E. Anduiza, A. Gallego, and M. Cantijoch, "Online Political Participation in Spain: The Impact of Traditional and Internet Resources," *Journal of Information Technology & Politics* 7: 4 (2010) 356–368.

R. Berry, G. Higgs, R. Fry, and M. Langford, "Web-Based GIS Approaches to Enhance Public Participation in Wind Farm Planning," *Transactions in GIS* 15: 2 (2011) 147–172.

G. Brown, "Public Participation GIS (PPGIS) for Regional and Environmental Planning: Reflections on a Decade of Empirical Research," *URISA Journal* 25: 2 (2012) 7–18.

G. Brown and S. Donovan, "Measuring Change in Place Values for Environmental and Natural Resource Planning Using Public Participation GIS (PPGIS): Results and Challenges for Longitudinal Research," *Society & Natural Resources* 27: 1 (2014) 36–54.

G. Brown and D. Weber, "Public Participation GIS: A New Method for National Park Planning," *Landscape and Urban Planning* 102: 1 (2011) 1–15.

G. Brown and D. Weber, "A Place-Based Approach to Conservation Management Using Public Participation GIS (PPGIS)," *Journal of Environmental Planning and Management* 56: 4 (2012) 455–473.

G. Brown, M. Kelly, and D. Whitall, "Which 'Public' Sampling Effects in Public Participation GIS (PPGIS) and Volunteered Geographic Information (VGI) Systems for Public Lands Management," *Journal of Environmental Planning and Management* 57: 2 (2013) 190–214.

G. Brown, J. Montag, and K. Lyon, "Public Participation GIS: A Method for Identifying Ecosystem Services," *Society & Natural Resources* 25: 7 (2014) 633–651.

N.R. Budhathoki, B. Bruce, and Z. Nedovic-Budic, "Reconceptualizing the Role of the User of Spatial Data Infrastructure," *GeoJournal* 72: 3 (2008) 149–160.

G. Bugs, C. Granell, O. Fonts, J. Huerta, and M. Painho, "An Assessment of Public Participation GIS and Web 2.0 Technologies in Urban Planning Practice in Canela, Brazil," *Cities* 27: 3 (2010) 172–181.

G. Curtin, "Free the Data!: E-Governance for Megaregions," *Public Works Management & Policy* 14: 3 (2010) 307–326.

W. Drummond and S. French, "The Future of GIS in Planning: Converging Technologies and Diverging Interests," *Journal of the American Planning Association* 74: 2 (2008) 161–174.

S. Elwood, "Volunteered Geographic Information: Future Research Directions Motivated by Critical, Participatory, and Feminist GIS," *GeoJournal* 72: 3 (2008a) 173–183.

S. Elwood, "Volunteered Geographic Information: Key Questions, Concepts and Methods to Guide Emerging Research and Practice," *GeoJournal* 72: 3 (2008b) 133–135.

J. Ferreira, "Comment on Drummond and French: GIS Evolution: Are we Messed up by Mashups?," *Journal of the American Planning Association* 74: 2 (2008) 177–179.

A. Flanagin and M. Metzger, "The Credibility of Volunteered Geographic Information," *GeoJournal* 72: 3 (2008) 137–148.

M. Goodchild, "Citizens as Sensors: The World of Volunteered Geography," *GeoJournal* 69: 4 (2007) 211–221.

E. Gordon, S. Schirra, and J. Hollander, "Immersive Planning: A Conceptual Model for Designing Public Participation with New Technologies," *Environment and Planning B: Planning and Design* 38 (2011) 505–519.

L. Harrie, S. Mustiere, and H. Stigmar, "Cartographic Quality Issues for View Services in Geoportals," *Cartographics* 46: 2 (2011) 92–100.

R. Klosterman, "The Politics of Computer-Aided Planning," *The Town Planning Review* 58: 4 (1987) 441–451.

R. Klosterman, "Comment on Drummond and French: Another View of the Future of GIS," *Journal of the American Planning Association* 74: 2 (2008) 174–176.

J. Krygier, "World Wide Web Mapping and GIS: An Application for Public Participation," *Cartographic Perspectives* 33 (1999) 66–67.

D.R. Lowery and W.C. Morse, "A Qualitative Method for Collecting Spatial Data on Important Places for Recreation, Livelihoods, and Ecological Meanings: Integrating Focus Groups with Public Participation Geographic Information Systems," *Society & Natural Resources* 26: 12 (2013) 1422–1437.

L. Mandarano, M. Meenar, and C. Steins, "Building Social Capital in the Digital Age of Civic Engagement," *Journal of Planning Literature* 25: 2 (2010) 123–135.

M.A. Pagano and A. Bowman, *Vacant Land in Cities: An Urban Resource* (Washington, D.C. Center on Urban and Metropolitan Policy, the Brookings Institution, 2000).

A. Pocewicz, G. Brown, M. Nielsen-Pincus, and R. Schnitzer, "An Evaluation of Internet Versus Paper-Based Methods for Public Participation Geographic Information Systems (PPGIS)," *Transactions in GIS* 16: 1 (2012) 39–53.

B. Resch and B. Zimmer, "User Experience Design in Professional Map-Based Geo-Portals," *ISPRS International Journal of Geo-Information* 2 (2013) 1015–1037.

M. Rhoads, "Face-to-Face and Computer-Mediated Communication: What does Theory Tell Us and what have we Learned so Far?," *Journal of Planning Literature* 25: 2 (2010) 111–122.

C. Rinner, C. Kebler, and S. Andrulis, "The Use of Web 2.0 Concepts to Support Deliberation in Spatial Decision-Making," *Computers, Environment and Urban Systems* 32: 5 (2008) 386–395.

C. Seeger, "The Role of Facilitated Volunteered Geographic Information in the Landscape Planning and Site Design Process," *GeoJournal* 72: 3 (2008) 199–213.

R. Sieber, "Public Participation Geographic Information Systems: A Literature Review and Framework," *Annals of the Association of American Geographers* 96 (2006) 491–507.

J.M. Thomas, "Targeting Strategies of Three Detroit CDCs," in M. Dewar and J.M. Thomas, eds., *The City after Abandonment* (Philadelphia, PA: University of Pennsylvania Press, 2013).

P. Wang, "Web-Based Public Participation GIS Application—A Case Study on Flood Emergency Management," Student thesis (Lund University, Department of Physical Geography and Ecosystem Science, 2012).

Appendix

Table A1: Sample of Data Portals

Name	Location	Website
Neighborhood Nexus	Atlanta, Georgia	http://www.neighborhoodnexus.org/
Baltimore Neighborhood Indicators Alliance	Baltimore, Maryland	http://www.bniajfi.org/
MetroBoston DataCommon	Boston, Massachusetts	http://www.metrobostondatacommon.org/
CAMConnect	Camden, New Jersey	http://www.camconnect.org/
Chattanooga—Ochs Center for Metropolitan Studies	Chattanooga, Tennessee	http://www.ochscenter.org/[1]
Chicago Metropolitan Agency for Planning	Chicago, Illinois	http://www.cmap.illinois.gov/
Cleveland—Center on Urban Poverty and community Development	Cleveland, Ohio	http://povertycenter.case.edu/
Columbus—Community Research Partners	Columbus, Ohio	http://www.communityresearchpartners.org/
Dallas—Institute for Urban Policy Research	Dallas, Texas	http://www.urbanpolicyresearch.org/
Denver—Piton Foundation	Denver, Colorado	http://www.piton.org/
Des Moines—United Way of Central Iowa	Des Moines, Iowa	http://www.unitedwaydm.org/
Des Moines—Child and Family Policy Center	Des Moines, Iowa	http://www.cfpciowa.org/
Detroit—Data Driven Detroit	Detroit, Michigan	http://datadrivendetroit.org/
Grand Rapids—Community Research Institute	Grand Rapids, Michigan	http://cridata.org/
HartfordInfo	Hartford, Connecticut	http://www.hartfordinfo.org/[1]
Indianapolis—The Polis Center	Indianapolis, Indian	http://www.polis.iupui.edu/
Indianapolis—United Way of Central Indiana Community Service Division	Indianapolis, Indian	http://www.uwci.org/
Kansas City—Center for Economic Information	Kansas City, Missouri	http://cei.umkc.edu/
Kansas City—the Mid-America Regional Council	Kansas City, Missouri	http://www.marc.org/
Miami—The Children's Trust	Miami, Florida	http://www.thechildrenstrust.org/

(Continued)

Table A1: Continued

Name	Location	Website
Minneapolis-St. Paul—Center for Urban and Regional Affairs	Minneapolis, Minnesota	http://www.cura.umn.edu
Twin Cities Compass	Minneapolis-St. Paul, Minnesota	http://www.mncompass.org/twincities/index.php
Minneapolis-St. Paul—Metropolitan Council/MetroGIS	Minneapolis-St. Paul, Minnesota	http://www.metrocouncil.org/Data-Maps/MetroGIS.aspx
Nashville—The Neighborhoods Resource Center	Nashville, Tennessee	http://www.gettingtowork.net/
New Haven—DataHaven	New Haven, Connecticut	http://www.ctdatahaven.org/
New Orleans—Greater New Orleans Community Data Center	New Orleans, Louisiana	http://www.gnocdc.org/
New York—New York City Housing and Neighborhood Information System	New York, New York	http://www.furmancenter.org/data/
Oakland—Urban Strategies Council	Oakland, California	http://www.infoalamedacounty.org/
Philadelphia—The Reinvestment Fund	Philadelphia, Pennsylvania	http://www.trfund.com/
Pittsburgh—The Pittsburgh neighborhood and Community Information Service	Pittsburgh, Pennsylvania	http://www.ucsur.pitt.edu/pncis.php
Portland—Institute of Portland Metropolitan Studies	Portland, Oregon	http://www.pdx.edu/ims/
Providence—The Providence Plan	Providence, Rhode Island	http://provplan.org/
St Louis—Rise/Neighborhood Data Gateway	St Louis, Missouri	http://www.datagateway.org/
San Antonio—Community Information Now	San Antonio, Texas	http://cinow.info/
Seattle—Public Health	Seattle, Washington	http://www.kingcounty.gov/healthservices/health.aspx
Washington—NeighborhoodInfo DC	Washington, DC	http://www.neighborhoodinfodc.org/
Washington—DC Local Initiative Support Corporation	Washington, DC	http://www.lisc.org/washington_dc/

Index

Note: page numbers in *italic* type refer to Figures; those in **bold** refer to Tables.

311 services 3, 78, 80–1; case study 82–91, **83**, *85*, **86**, **87**, **88**

adversarial design 11
age: and e-government 84; and social media use 65, 69
agents (technology-assisted participatory platforms) 30, *30*, 32
agonistic spaces 17
Apps for Development 42, 43
ARC (Applied Research Collaborative) 127, 133
Arnold, M. 69–70
Arnstein ladder of public participation 28–9, 45, 45–6
artifacts, as alternative forms of publishing scholarship 13
attractors (technology-enabled participatory platforms) 30, *30*, 31
Austin; SpeakUpAustin 41, 42

Bell, G. 18
Betaville 9–10
Bhagwatwar, Akshay 25–50
black box of technology 7, 8, 18, 20
Bloomfield, Pittsburgh; online event information study 101–21
borders 2
Boston; codesign workshops 2, 10–11, 14–16, 20
boyd, dinah 53, 55, 71
Brown, G. 128–9, 135
Brusilovsky, Peter 95–123
Budhathoki, N.R. 131
Bugs, G. 127
Butler, Brian 3, 95–123

C2G (citizen-to-government) communication 79
C2G2C (citizen-to-government-to-citizen) communication 3, 78, 80
Calgary; neighborhood associations 54
Calvino, Italo 17

Carson, Kathleen 4, 125–39
Cavallo, Sara 3, 77–93
Center for Social Innovation, Toronto 12
Change by Us Philly 37
Chicago: codesign workshops 2, 10–11, 14–16, 17, 19, 20; Crime in Chicago 32
cities *see* urban areas
citizen control (Arnstein ladder of public participation) 29, 45, *45*
citizen power (Arnstein ladder of public participation) 29, *45*, 45–6
citizen science 15
citizen-centric and citizen-sourced data (technology-enabled participatory platforms) 2, 37, **38**, 40, 44, **45**, *45*
citizen-centric and government open data (technology-enabled participatory platforms) 2, **39**, 40–1, 44, **45**, *45*
citizen-to-government (C2G) communication 79
citizen-to-government-to-citizen (C2G2C) communication 3, 78, 80
civic engagement 25–6; definition of 28; and technology 28–9 *see also* Designing Policy project; technology-enabled participatory platforms
civic pride, and local events 97
CKAN (Open Knowledge Foundation) 133
clustering exercises 12
code / space 9
codescapes 9
codesign workshops/toolkit *see* Designing Policy project
Coffin, Sarah L. 4, 125–39
cognitive surplus 28
communities of interest 53
Connected City illustrations (iStock) 13–14
consultation (Arnstein ladder of public participation) 28–9, 45, *45*
Crank, L. 55
Crime in Chicago 32
critical design 11

141

INDEX

crowdfunding/crowdsourcing 26
Crutcher, M. 89

Dancygier, Aaron 40
data democratization 135
data patchworking 130–1
delegated power (Arnstein ladder of public participation) 29, 45, *45*
design: and prototyping 8–9, 16, 17, 18–19, 20; speculative design 8–9, 11; and values 9–10, 16, 17–18, 20
design fiction 11, 14, 16
design frictions, in participatory design 17–19, 20
designers, role of 19
Designing Policy project 7–11, 20; background to 11–12; codesign workshops 2, 3, 10–11, 14–16; and design frictions 17–19, 20; future implications 19–20; toolkit 2, 12–14
Desouza, Kevin C. 2–3, 25–50
digital divide: and e-government 3, 78, 81; and social media 64–6, 67, 69, 71; and technology-enabled participatory platforms 46
Dilworth, Richard 1–5
Dourish, P. 2, 18
Drummond, W. 126, 134–5

e-government 3, 78–80; 311 services case study 82–91, **83**, *85*, **86**, **87**, **88**
E-Government Act of 2002 77, 81
East Liberty, Pittsburgh; online event information study 101–21
East-West Gateway Council of Governments 127, 130
Ellison, N. 55
Elwood, S. 130
environmental crises 15
events, local, information about 95–101; online information study 101–21

Facebook; Indian Hills Neighbourhood Association (INHA), social media study 3, 53, 56–71, *57, 58,* **59, 63**
Flanagin, A. 130
Flash Mob Ethnography 12
flows (technology-enabled participatory platforms) 30, *30*, 31
for-profit institutions, and local event information 112, **112**, 113, **113**, *113*, **114**, 119, 120
Forlano, Laura 2, 3, 7–24
Forte, Andrea 1–5
Foth, M. 70
French, S. 126, 134–5

G2C (government-to-citizen) communication 79

Ganning, Joana P. 4, 125–39
Gaved, M. 70
gender; and urban design 17
GeoNode 133–4
Geoportal Server (ESRI) 133
geoportals 126–7; open-source geoportal software 133 *see also* regional data portals
GeoWeb 77, 91
GIS systems *see* PPGIS (public participation GIS); regional data portals
goals (technology-enabled participatory platforms) 30, *30*, 31–2
Goodchild, M. 77–8
Gordon, E. 135
government organizations, and local event information 112, **112**, 113, **113**, *113*
government-centric and citizen-developed solutions (technology-enabled participatory platforms) 2–3, **39**, 42–3, 44, **45**, *45*, 45–6
government-centric and citizen-sourced data (technology-enabled participatory platforms) 2, **39**, 41–2, 44, 45, *45*
government-to-citizen (G2C) communication 79
Grow a Game project 10
Guest, A. M. 54

Halegoua, Germaine R. 3, 51–75
Hampton, K. 55.56, 81
Harrison, S. 2
health care; technologies of the body 15
Highland Park, Pittsburgh; online event information study 101–21
Hillgren, P.-A. 17
Hillier, J. 53–4
Hollander, J. 135
Hub2 9–10

Indian Hills Neighbourhood Association (INHA), social media study 56–71, *57, 58,* **59, 63**
information; definition of 31
informing (Arnstein ladder of public participation) 28, 29, *45*
internet of things 15
iStock 13–14
iStrategyLabs 42, 43

Johnson, Bonnie J. 3, 51–75

Kansas Transportation Online Community (K-TOC) 41, 42
Klosterman, R. 128, 131, 135
knowledge, definition of 31
Kotler, M. 54
Krygier, J. 128
Kundra, Vivek 42

INDEX

Lawrence, Kansas *see* Indian Hills Neighbourhood Association (INHA), social media study
local event information 95–101; online sources study 3, 101–21
localocracy 37
López, Claudia 3, 95–123
Lynch, Joann 77–93

Mathew, Anijo 2, 3, 7–24
McCall, Benjamin 4, 125–39
media, traditional, and local events information 98–101, 107–8
mediums (technology-enabled participatory platforms) 30, *30,* 31
Metzger, M. 130
Migurski, Mike 40
minority populations, and e-government 84, 89
Monti, D. J. 54
Mouffe, Chantal 17

neighborhood associations 54; Indian Hills Neighbourhood Association (INHA), social media study 56–71, *57, 58,* **59, 63**; and social media 3, 52–3
neighborhoods 3, 53–5; and digital communication 55–6; local event information 95–121; and participatory design 16
neogeography 78, 90–1
Netville 55
networked publics 53
New York: 311 services 3, 78, 82–91, **83,** *85,* **86, 87, 88**; Big Apps competition 26–7, 40, 41, 42–3; codesign workshops 2, 10–11, 14–16, 20; NYC Health Ratings website 40, 41
newspaper media, and local events information 98–101, 107–8
non-participation (Arnstein ladder of public participation) 28, *45*
not-for-profit institutions, and local event information 112, **112,** 113, **113,** *113,* **114,** 119, 120
NYC Health Ratings website 40, 41

Oakland Crimespotting app 40, 41
OneSTL 127
online event information 101–21
Open Data Catalogue (ODC, Azavea) 133
open-source geoportal software 133

Pachube.com 15
participatory design 8–9, 10–11; design frictions in 17–19 *see also* Designing Policy project
partnership (Arnstein ladder of public participation) 29, *45,* 45–6

Pattavina, A. 55
Philadelphia; Change by Us Philly 37
Pigg, K. 55
Pittsburgh Post-Gazette 98–101, 103, **105,** 105–6, **106,** 110, **110,** 111, 113, **115**
Pittsburgh, PA; local event information study 96–121
placation (Arnstein ladder of public participation) 29, 45, *45*
place, definition of 2
planning information *see* regional data portals
population, urban 1
PPGIS (public participation GIS) 126, 134–6; overview and survey 128–34, **132**
prototyping, and design 8–9, 16, 17, 18–19, 20

regional data portals 4, 125–6; case study 127–36; terminology and definitions 126–7
religious organizations, and local event information 112, **112,** 113, **113,** *113*
Rodousakis, N. 84
Royal College of Art 11

San Francisco: 311 services 3, 78, 82–91, **83,** *85,* **86, 87, 88**; Oakland Crimespotting app 40, 41
Schirra, S. 135
Scull, Peter 77–93
Seattle; neighborhood associations 54
Simmel, Georg 17
simulations 9–10
situated technologies 9
Smart Cities 7–8
social media: complaints about 67; Indian Hills Neighbourhood Association (INHA), social media study 3, 53, 56–71, *57, 58,* **59, 63**
socio-demographic factors; 311 services study **83,** 83–4, **87–8,** 89–90
socio-political values 9–10
space, definition of 2
SpeakUpAustin 41, 42
speculative design 8–9, 11
sponsors, and local events information 106–7
Squirrel Hill, Pittsburgh; online event information study 101–21
St Louis Regional Data Exchange 126, 127, 129, 130, 131, 133–4 *see also* regional data portals
St. Nicks Alliance 11
Stamen Design 40
Stephens, M. 84
Streib, G. 84
Superstorm Sandy 15
sustainability planning 129

INDEX

Symposium on Urban Informatics 1, 2, 4
systems theory 29–30

technological capabilities (technology-enabled participatory platforms) 30, *30*, 31
technologies of the body 15
technology-enabled participatory platforms 2–3, 26–8, 29–32, *30*; four archetypes of 32, 37, **38–9,** 40–7, *45*; list of platforms **33–6**
Textizen 26, 30–2
third wave e-gov (c2g2c) 3, 78, 80
Thomas, J. 84
tokenism (Arnstein ladder of public participation) 28–9, 45, *45*
Turner, A. 78
Twitter; Indian Hills Neighbourhood Association (INHA), social media study 3, 53, 56–71, *57, 58,* **59,** 63

Unger, D. G. 54
universities; institutional review boards (IRBs) 19
Unsworth, Kristene 1–5

urban advertising 17
urban clusters; classification of 1
urban informatics: classification of 1; definition of 1–2
Urban Mechanics 29
urban screens 15, 17
urban technology, and value-sensitive design 9–10
urbanized areas; classification of 1
UrbanSim 9–10

values, and design 9–10, 16, 17–18, 20
Van Aerschot, L. 83, 84
volunteered geographic information (VGI) 3, 77–8, 80, 127, 130, 134, 135; case study 82–91, **83,** *85,* **86, 87, 88**

Wandersman, A. 54
Washington, DC; 311 services 3, 78, 82–91, **83,** *85,* **86, 87, 88**
Web 2.0 77, 78, 79
Weiser, Mark 18
Wellman, B. 55, 81

Zook, M. 89